THE EARLY FICTION OF PHILIP ROTH

Dr. Balbir Singh

OMEGA PUBLICATIONS
NEW DELHI 110002 (INDIA)

OMEGA PUBLICATIONS
4398/5, Ansari Road, Daryaganj,
New Delhi-110 002
Phone: 65901906
e-mail: omega_publications@yahoo.com

Head Office :
79/3, Laxmi Garden,
Near Satya Jyoti School,
Gurgaon (Haryana)
Mob.: 9811787417

The Early Fiction of Philip Roth

First Published, 2009

ISBN-978-81-8455-112-9

PRINTED IN INDIA

Printed at Tarun Offset Printer Delhi - 110053

Preface

Philip Roth is one of the most significant contemporary American novelists. After writing more than twenty odd books he is still engaged in creative activities. He has been honored with various prestigious literary awards.

The most important and interesting aspect of Roth's fiction is his preoccupation with manners and morals of contemporary society, in other words, the business of living in this postmodern world where the hero of Bellow's *Dangling Man* asks: "How should a good man live, what ought he to do?" He will definitely secure a place in a Leavisian tradition if such a tradition ever exists in American literary history. Roth is a volatile writer who has written short stories, a play, novels and critical essays. So it is not feasible to study in detail all his fiction. Therefore, I have limited myself exclusively to his earlier work, and even among them those novels where he is most solemnly and profoundly occupied with moral values. But these selected books will substantially bring about his essential ethical vision and point of view.

I frankly admit that the book is based on my doctoral research work. I hope that the present work will pave the way for further research in Rothian scholarship.

Dr. Balbir Singh

Contents

Contents

1
Introduction

If we cast a cursory glance on postwar American fiction we shall observe a tremendous change in themes as well as techniques. The predominant contemporary writers display a sharp diversion from the literary tradition followed by the writers in the early decades of the twentieth century. Before the Second World War the literary scene in America was dominated by such writers as John Dos Passos, John Steinbeck and Ernest Hemingway. They had a firm belief in the progress of humanity towards a definite and affirmative goal though their lamentation for the loss of old moral values was genuine. Characteristically, a few of them were war veterans who had witnessed meaningless violence on the battlefront and had lost faith in the social and political establishment. But even in the realistic and naturalistic fiction of the twenties and the thirties, the protagonist was found to be engaged in a heroic struggle to achieve selfhood and identity in the middle of unmanning and dehumanizing forces. The legendary hero of Hemingway wages his heroic and relentless battle against the forces of evil, decadence, and annihilation, and, eventually, achieves at least a moral victory even though he is defeated in worldly terms. Though the old values were being replaced by the new ones, the writer still projected a vision of society as a source of vitality, moral nourishment and support. The fictional hero, though disillusioned with the falsehood and hypocrisy around him, still operated in his social world to justify and affirm his existence.

However, in the fiction of the forties and the fifties a drastic change of emphasis could be observed. Though writers like Hemingway and William Faulkner were still writing actively, a new generation of American writers was fast emerging for whom the external reality had assumed a new form and meaning. These writers found their imaginative sensibility inadequate to encompass the existential reality confronting them. The hero of prewar realistic fiction was gradually replaced by a new figure who finds himself grossly ill-equipped to vanquish the strange and hostile forces surrounding him. He seems to have lost faith in his capacity to encounter the onslaught of the anonymous and destructive powers governing his destiny. Consequently, instead of fighting a heroic battle to affirm his dignity and manliness he finds himself trapped in and victimized by the dehumanizing environment around him. The protagonist in such novels as Saul Bellow's *The Victim*, Ralph Ellison's *Invisible Man*, and Norman Mailer's *The Naked and the Dead* finds himself in a grim and absurd situation. Divested of his glory and dignity, he is found grappling with incomprehensible and hitherto unknown forces bent upon stripping him of his identity and essential humanity. The contemporary writer, thus, is trying to explore in his fiction what Malcolm Bradbury calls "the predicament of disoriented modern man in a world of urban anonymity, behavioral indifference, and the totalitarian massing of social force".[1] He seems to be convinced that in a world where normative social values hold sway it is difficult to assert human values.

The contemporary novelist seems to be so acutely aware of the individual's loss of identity in a baffling and confounding reality that Ellison does not even give a name to his protagonist in *Invisible Man*. The hero is engaged in a battle for survival as a human entity, though he is acutely conscious of the futility of setting even such meager aims. At the most, he achieves only moral victory at the end of his encounters and explorations. The inhuman and the mechanized system not only crushes him but also deprives him of any concrete opportunity to register even his human identity. Tony Tanner exactly evokes the image of this new kind of hero: "Clay, jelly, jelly-fish – what this image cluster suggests is the dread of utter formlessness, of being a soft, vulnerable, endlessly manipulable blob, of not being a distinct self".[2] The central character of this fiction is unable to grasp the nature of the component forces of the existential reality, let alone overcome them. Not surprisingly, the modern novelist finds it difficult to give shape to the chaotic and bizarre experience bombarding his artistic sensibility. Commenting on the incoherent and discordant nature of contemporary reality, Philip Roth says in *Reading Myself and Others* :

> The American writer in the middle of the twentieth century has his hands full in trying to understand, describe, and then make credible much of American reality. It stupefies, it sickens, it infuriates, and finally it is even a kind of embarrassment to one's own meager imagination.[3]

It is not, therefore, surprising that the postwar novelist in search of new fictional techniques is turning to more and more experimentation.

The most unpleasant offshoot of this absurdism and nihilism becomes manifest in the helpless passivity on the part of the individual. Unable to find any viable sustenance in the recognizable social world, he isolates himself from this world and withdraws into his own lonely self; in Ihab Hassan's words, he "recoils" in himself.[4] In this way a new kind of hero – the "anti-hero" or the "rebel-victim" comes into being who is in search for "existential fulfillment, that is, freedom and self-definition".[5] But instead of achieving recognition of his existence, he finds himself alienated and isolated from his recognizable social world. John N. McDaniel is of the opinion that there are "two essential modes of existential response – active self-assertion and passive victimization" in the contemporary American fiction and that these modes are embodied by two types of heroes, the assertive figure and the victim figure.[6] Combining these two types of heroes in a single paradoxical figure, "rebel-victim", Hassan asserts that the two modes are opposite facets of the same reaction of withdrawal from society.[7]

In Saul Bellow's *Seize the Day*, for instance, the protagonist Tommy Wilhelm is a typical victim of dehumanizing social forces. Similarly, contemporary writers like Thomas Pynchon, Joseph Heller, J.D. Salinger, Bernard Malamud, and Kurt Vonnegut, Jr. have created characters who seem to be operating outside the orbit of society. Instead of active engagement in the social process with a view to manage the outer forces to his advantage, the new hero is found to be drifting passively in a social vacuum. Instead of growing in the ambience of society, he functions within the recesses of his own self. The dichotomy in social and individual values forces him to turn inward to his own inner resources to compensate his moral loss. Pointing out the characteristic isolation of the American hero from the larger society, Walter Allen observes: "They are characters not in process of discovering the nature of society and of themselves in and through society but are, on the contrary, characters profoundly alienated from society".[8] They seem to have lost their interest in social and moral processes and are tempted to escape into an unreal and fantastic world devoid of the pain which they confront in society.

As a matter of fact, the awareness of this process of recoil from society is more poignant and intense in the postwar Jewish-American fiction. These writers, most of them second generation immigrants to America, have inherited the bitter memories of the victimization of their forefathers in Europe consequent upon the Holocaust. They have witnessed the frantic struggle of their parents in the new environment to fulfill the cherished American dream of success. Owing to their ethnic and historical background, their parents had to face multifarious conflicts in this new land. Basically they were intellectual people, highly interested in reading and writing books. They had a natural inner urge to express the pain of separation from their past and the problems and needs of assimilation in an alien, though, affluent society. The earlier Jewish writers of the immigrant generation were preoccupied more with the themes of economic and social security. The best known work of this period is Abraham Cahan's *The Rise of David Levinsky* which deals with the problem of assimilation of the ghetto Jews. But after the Second World War the Jewish intellectuals had started sharing the American prosperity and establishing themselves in their new environment. In fact, the response of the postwar Jewish-American writers (who were by now more or less assimilated middle-class Americans) to the secular and prosperous American society is more complex.

The protagonist in Jewish-American fiction is, more often than not, a figure who is as much a victim of an alien and antagonistic society as of his own foolishness and anxieties. Saul Bellow's Leventhal, Philip Roth's Sabbath, and Bernard Malamud's Harry – all represent the typical Jewish hero who is characterized by his sense of moral rectitude, worldly failure, intense suffering and absurd behavior. There is a near unanimity in the critical opinion that the plight of the Jew represents the predicament of the modern man. The characters of many Jewish-American novelists experience the feelings of rootlessness, loneliness, alienation and marginalization – the symptoms of what Mark Shechner calls "The Modern Condition".[9] In this respect, the fiction of all major Jewish-American novelists like Bellow, Malamud, Gold, Mailer and Roth encompasses the broader humanitarian concerns. The typical Jewish figure, *schlemiel*, which emerges from the contemporary Jewish-American fiction is characterized by his stoicism, fortitude and the pre-eminence of moral sense. He has also the ability to laugh at his bizarre and absurd circumstances. Ruth Wisse remarks that *schlemiel* in Jewish-American fiction tries to prove "his humanity by loving and suffering in defiance of the forces of depersonalization and the ethic of enlightened stoicism".[10] In the process, he does manage to evolve some ingenious survival strategies which define both his survival instincts and his moral and ethical vision.

Philip Roth, Saul Bellow and Bernard Malamud have a distinct voice in the contemporary American fiction inasmuch as they analyze ethical aspects of the predicament of modern man in the context of his family and society. Together they constitute a fictional voice which calls for the need of assertion of basic human values in dealing with the individual response to the compulsion of survival in the existential reality. In their investigation of the human condition, they infuse in their fiction all of their experience imbibed from their native Judaic tradition as well as from the diverse fields of human activities in the secular society of America. Consequently, their fictional meaning extends beyond the narrow confines of Jewish sensibility to the universal human condition.

Philip Roth, more than the other two, believes in the

role of society as the sole medium for the self in its moral quest. His insistence that the contemporary writer should strive more to explore the social world clearly indicates his firm conviction that man's growth cannot be ensured in social and moral vacuum and he has to operate in the tangible social world to achieve his aim of self-fulfillment and self-affirmation. Beginning his literary career with *Goodbye, Columbus and Five Short Stories* in 1959, he has to his credit more than twenty novels besides his autobiography, short stories and critical essays. Roth has been a controversial writer ever since he published his first book, which evoked a mixed response. Some critics praised the novella *Goodbye, Columbus* and other short stories for their freshness, originality and energy, and hailed Roth as a promising young writer. He was, on the other hand, assailed by some critics and the Rabbis for portraying the Jews disparagingly. Nevertheless, the book won the 1960 National Book Award for Fiction. Since then a number of critical books and essays have appeared examining closely the diverse implications of the fictional art of Philip Roth.

Many Jewish critics and the Rabbis, as mentioned earlier, came down heavily upon Roth for his anti-Semitic views and branded him a self-hating Jew. Jeremy Larner complained that Roth is striving to "cheapen the people he writes about".[11] Irving Howe praised him for his insight and imagination but later dismissed him saying that he is a "minor writer" who has "denied himself, programmatically, the vision of major possibilities".[12] This disapproval took the form of a fierce controversy after the publication of *Portnoy's Complaint*, the novel which made Roth a successful, rich and even notorious figure overnight. On the other hand, critics like Theodore Solotaroff praised him lavishly for his emphasis on traditional Jewish values. He finds the charge of anti-Semitism and self-hatred leveled upon Roth as unfounded and absurd. He remarks in this context: "The directness of his attack against arrogance, smugness, finagling, and acquisitiveness should not obscure the perfectly obvious fact that he does so flying a traditional Jewish banner of sentiment and humaneness and personal responsibility...."[13] This view is supported by critics like Ben Siegel who feel that Roth along with his contemporaries like Bellow, Malamud, Salinger and Gold has compensated the loss of religious concerns with deep commitment to Judaic values.

But this view is as one-sided as the former charge of anti-Semitism and does not describe sufficiently the moral stance of Philip Roth who has time and again declared that his artistic creed is not limited by any narrow ethnic considerations. Roth has repeatedly tried to defend himself in various interviews, seminars and critical essays regarding the charge of ethnicity. Responding to his detractors, he says in *Reading Myself and Others*:

> Not only do they seem to me often to have cramped and untenable notions of right and wrong, but looking at fiction as they do – in terms of 'approval' and 'disapproval' of Jews, 'positive' and 'negative' attitudes toward Jewish life – they are likely not to see what it is that the story is really about.[14]

Roth has an intimate and exhaustive knowledge of Jewish culture and tradition which provides him with the essential fictional material out of which he moulds his fiction. In the range and scope of his fiction, he is not confined to any narrow ethnic tradition though he draws upon his personal experience as a Jew in the American society. Referring to adultery committed by Epstein in the story of the same title when somebody asked him whether it was a Jewish trait, he replied: "It is a decidedly human possibility".[15]

Though Roth's fictional world is largely inhabited by Jewish characters, his approach in dealing with their psychological and moral problems is essentially secular and universal. Moreover, in such novels as *When She Was Good* and *The Great American Novel* he has rendered the Mid-West Protestant milieu as forcefully and convincingly as Jewish society. Far from being anti-Semitic or a self-flagellating Jew, he is actually proud of his Jewish heritage. He proclaims in *Reading Myself and Others*: "... I have always been far more pleased by my good fortune in being born a Jew than my critics may begin to imagine".[16] Although he seems to share with some of his contemporary Jewish writers the belief that "the Jewish character is one that places a premium on generosity, abstinence, concern, responsibility, and civilization," he nowhere hints that these virtues are in any way prerogatives of the Jews.[17] Thus, it can be safely concluded that Jewish milieu and characters are a medium for Roth through which he projects his vision of human condition. His ethical and social concerns though rooted in the particularities of Jewish life extend outwardly to the general humanity. Most of the critics agree that Roth naturally belongs to the essential Jewish-American tradition of Bellow, Malamud, Salinger, Mailer and Gold in his treatment of individual experience in contemporary American society. But he is distinct from them at least in one important respect, viz. his deep commitment to family and society. In this respect, George J. Searles finds him closer to John Updike, a non-Jewish writer.

The earliest and the most comprehensive critical study of Roth's fiction has been undertaken by John N. McDaniel. Placing Roth in the Jewish-American tradition of Bellow, Malamud, Salinger and Gold, McDaniel believes that like his contemporaries Roth deals with the subject of "the self in society" and his vision of self is deeply embedded in the familial and social matrix.[18] McDaniel discerns two types of behavioral patterns in Roth's characters in their response to the existential reality, "active self-assertion" and "passive victimization".[19] Following this criterion, he divides his main characters into two broad categories corresponding to their attitude. Ozzie Freedman of "The Conversion of the Jews", Eli Peck of "Eli, the Fanatic", Neil Klugman of *Goodbye Columbus,* and Gabe Wallach of *Letting Go* are considered to be in the activist mode refusing to be victimized and striving vehemently to assert the self even after being thwarted by the hostile outside forces. Lou Epstein of "Epstein", Novotany in "Novotany's Pain", Libby Herz of *Letting Go,* Lucy Nelson of *When She Was Good,* and Portnoy of *Portnoy's Complaint* are passive sufferers who feel helpless and victimized at the hands of the outer reality and tolerate their condition or attempt to reconcile with their predicament. He concludes that in the course of Roth's fiction there is a subtle but significant shift from the activist mode to the absurdist mode. Similarly, Tony Tanner finds two major impulses in Roth's fiction: the first is a desire to understand the self, and the second is an effort to observe the familial and the social. In *Portnoy's Complaint,* according to him, these impulses seem to be "coalesced".[20]

Judith Paterson Jones and Guinevera A. Nance are of the opinion that Roth is "an incisive observer of the American social and political scene" and his fiction takes up the problem of authority over individual life.[21] This, in turn, generates various kinds of conflicts which take different forms in different novels. The conflict is between children and parents in *Goodbye, Columbus, When She Was Good and Portnoy's Complaint,* between male and female in *My Life as a Man,* between passion and restraint in *The Professor of Desire,* and between art and personal experience in his later autobiographical books. They conclude that Roth portrays a "secularized society that takes its religion where it can ... and points to the universalities of the human condition that lie beneath the secular facade".[22]

Hermione Lee in her brief but incisive study traces the origin of Roth's fiction in three main currents of English literature : black surrealism of the thirties, Jewish-American tradition of the forties and the fifties dominated by moral seriousness and the aspiration of the self in an alien Gentile world, and the European tradition of Franz Kafka and Nikolai Gogol. In her opinion, the Rothian protagonist, who is often an educated and intelligent middle class urbanite, is found "attempting to break through some prevention or blockage, to 'crash through the wall' into a free, full sense of self".[23] This blockage may take the form of an over-protected guilty childhood, discordant marriage or love affair, and his efforts to change his life or to learn to live with his condition. She tries to relate this personal experience to the disillusioning experience of American psyche from its primeval innocence of the fifties to the demythologizing sixties and seventies.

Mark Shechner attempts to analyze the predicament of Roth's characters from psychological point of view. According to him, Roth shares with his contemporary novelists the prevalent belief in what he calls "ethical Jewhood", the myth of association of a Jew with such moral virtues as generosity, responsibility, sacrifice and stoicism.[24] He calls Roth a genuine "novelist of manners" which, in his case, reflect the despair, frustrations and longings of his characters.[25] Because of the energy and intensity of emotions, *My Life As a Man* is considered by him the best novel of Roth whereas *The Professor of Desire* is deemed not to be so successful. In his opinion, the situations in which his characters find themselves "may be comical or grim, but at their most interesting are comically grim."[26] The peculiar brand of humor found in his fiction emerges from the pain which lies beneath the comic surface. Though illuminating, Shechner's views remain essentially psychological.

George J. Searles in his comparative study of the fiction of Roth and Updike underlines the similarities of their major themes. Roth, like Updike, deals with the theme of "ethnic identity, family relationships, individual moral responsibility and guilt, sexuality and romantic love, materialism, and social mores in general."[27] He also observes in Roth's fiction a kind of tension between the traditional European Jewishness and the secularized modern experience of the assimilated Jews in America. Allen Guttmann in his essay "Philip Roth and the Rabbis" examines the conflict between the Jewish tradition and the process of assimilation in the Gentile American society, and finally comes to the conclusion that Roth is a "thoroughly assimilated American writer".[28] His views are apparently shared by Murray Baumgarten and Barbara Gottfried who in their comprehensive study of Roth's fiction opine that his fiction displays the predicament of the Jewish characters who are in the process of assimilation in the American society. "In their desperate quest for selfhood," they observe, "his Jewish characters echo the experiences of the classic American heroes...."[29]

Though a number of critics have attempted to examine the comic vision of Roth, it is Jay L. Halio who has undertaken a detailed and comprehensive study of his fiction with a view to demonstrate his capabilities and achievements as a "specifically comic writer".[30] He has elaborately dwelt upon Roth's comic and satirical techniques. Halio indicates in Roth's fiction the presence of the traditional figure of schlemiel, the typical suffering Jew, who manages to survive amidst adverse circumstances. Through the comic medium, his fiction depicts the struggle of his characters to strike a balance between their Jewish heritage and the new American environment. They are generally placed in difficult circumstances trying to search for some solution. By focusing on the distortions brought about in their personality as a result of their inapt handling of the crises in their lives, Roth not only creates humor but also portrays moral conflicts in the American society. No doubt, on some occasions, Roth displays a flair for creating absurd and fantastical situations, but they are exclusively meant for creating comic effects or conveying his moral indignation at the social or political hypocrisy and are in no way comparable to those bizarre and absurdly comic situations frequently found in recent American literature. The absurdist mode in Roth's fiction becomes a technique of comedy and satire and not an escape route for the anguished self.

Roth has been criticized by some feminine critics for portraying women in a disparaging manner. In her essay on some of the major female characters in the early fiction of Roth, Mary Allen observes that Roth's women have been found to exert their power over their male counterparts. They appear to be destructive creatures who are bent upon crushing the males who dominate them. In her opinion, Roth shows them lacking in those magnanimous and noble qualities which his male characters wish them to possess. She further observes : "And yet Roth's heroines do lack the quality that seems most important to him – genuine goodness."[31] But the charge of anti-feminism on Roth seems to be as unfounded and one-sided as that of anti-Semitism. On close scrutiny, it will be discerned that in his fiction weaknesses of men are projected through the viewpoints of women. Moreover, the females are also engaged in their struggle to affirm their identity and selfhood amidst the existential reality. Even the charge of lack of goodness in Roth's female characters does not hold much water in case of such heroines as Claire Ovington in *The Professor of Desire*. The problem with Allen's assessment of Roth's female characters is that it is made only on the basis of his novels *Portnoy's Complaint, Letting Go* and *When She Was Good*. In some of his later novels, Roth certainly presents such female characters who are capable of "eliciting our deepest sympathies."[32]

From the above discussion it is clear that most of the critics agree that Roth's basic concerns are with individual in society. The predicament and concerns of the Rothian protagonists in coping with the familial and societal pressures form the nucleus of major criticism of Roth's fiction. But somehow a majority of critical studies fail to ignore the Jewish milieu while examining the individual's response to social reality. As has already been discussed, the modern reality is so oppressive that the individual finds it difficult to affirm his faith in normative value system of society. The hero in Roth's fiction is highly conscious of his own ethical values imbibed instinctively from his inherited culture and tradition, and his experience in a secular society. He finds these values to be in opposition to the normative values imposed upon him by his surrounding society. To ensure his survival as a human entity, he has to choose from the limited options available to him. He may conform to the demands of the society; he may rebel against it and become an outcast; or he can choose to become a "victim" which, according to Hassan, amounts to the same thing.[33] Alternatively, he may try to escape in a romantic and imaginary world of his own construction or in a paranoid void. Lastly, he may attempt to achieve a kind of reconciliation by modifying the mechanism of his response to the outer reality. Tommy Wilhelm in Bellow's *Seize the Day* feels alienated and victimized in a dehumanizing social system and is only able to bring about "the consummation of his heart's ultimate need"[34] through an emotional understanding of the working of the existential forces. The hero of Ellison's *Invisible Man* goes underground after a sustained battle against the ruthlessly cruel system and waits hopefully for moral regeneration. Bellow's Herzog tries to compensate his loss of innocence by comprehending the mysterious relationship of self and the existential reality.

Unlike many of the contemporary heroes who display a tendency to avoid society, Roth's characters are conscious of the desirability of active self-assertion in the face of moral challenges. They are invariably driven by a compelling sense of moral obligation to their society and to themselves. Malcolm Bradbury is of the opinion that in Roth's earlier fiction the hero struggles between "traditional ethics and new narcissistic desires for personal freedom".[35] His characters are not fatalistic and deterministic; rather, as he himself admits in *Reading Myself and Others*, "the business of choosing is the primary occupation of any number of my characters".[36] Neil Klugman and Brenda Patimkin in *Goodbye, Columbus;* Gabe Wallach, Libby Herz and Paul Herz in *Letting Go;* Peter Tarnopol in *My Life as a Man;* David Kepesh in *The Professor of Desire;* Alexander Portnoy in *Portnoy's Complaint*, and other major characters in his fiction are not merely puppets in the hands of a supreme fate but meet their destiny through a conscious and deliberate choice. Reacting to the charge that his vision of life is fatalistic, he says in *Reading Myself and Others* that far from being deterministic his protagonist invariably makes

> a conscious, deliberate, even willful choice beyond the boundary lines of his life, and just so as to give expression to what in his spirit will not be grimly determined, by others, or even by what he had himself taken to be his own nature.[37]

For Roth, literature is a "matter of moral significance".[38] Even the process of writing fiction is a form of ethical conduct or, perhaps, even the way to a good life. Particularly in the early phase of his career, he was so dedicated to the notion of ethical function of literature and to what Lionel Trilling calls "moral realism",[39] that he thought of "fiction to be something like a religious calling and literature a kind of sacrament."[40] He was especially influenced by such realistic writers as Henry James, Thomas Mann, Anton Chekhov and Gustave Flaubert. The strong moral strain prevalent in their fiction reinforced his belief that literature has a high moral purpose and a liberating force for the writer as well as the reader. McDaniel rightly links him with the moral tradition of novelists like Henry James, Leo Tolostoy and Joseph Conrad. "For Roth", he remarks in this context, "as for James, fiction not only treats moral issues, but has the purpose of elevating and liberating the reader's social and moral consciousness....[41] Though his ethical stance is consistent, in his early novels like *Letting Go, When She Was Good and My Life as a Man* he explicitly and passionately relates social experience with moral values. At this stage, writing fiction itself was considered by him as equivalent to an ethical activity which could inspire the artist to ennoble his own life and persuade the reader as well to involve in the moral process. Peter Tarnopol in *My Life as a Man* is firmly convinced that literature would somehow liberate him from his predicament and lead him to the path of salvation. The mysterious relationship of Libby and Gabe in *Letting Go* begins through a copy of Henry James's *The Portrait of a Lady*. Even in his comic works like *Our Gang* and *The Great American Novel*, he probes moral issues which have a bearing on the contemporary social and moral problems. Pointing out the moral purpose of his satires, Roth observes: "Satire is moral rage transformed into comic art – as an elegy is grief transformed into poetic art".[42]

In his fiction Philip Roth is preoccupied with the fundamental problem of survival of the individual in modern society which seems to be bereft of basic human values like justice, love and human sympathy. The society demands conformity to its normative values denying, at the same time, any freedom to the individual to fulfill his aspirations. Roth depicts in his fiction the conflict between an instinctive urge of the individual to uphold sublime moral values and the suffocating weight of the forces of normalcy. This conflict assumes different forms in different novels. In his attempt to trace the journey of the self through the labyrinth of moral barrenness and sterility to its cherished goal he is solely guided, it may be explicitly stated, by humanitarian values as perceived and imbibed by the heart. The Yiddish proverb used by Roth as the epigraph of *Goodbye, Columbus* "The heart is half a prophet", sums up the core of his ethical vision. Instead of any logical principles or theories of any school of philosophy, the truth perceived instinctively through the heart can lead the individual to salvation.

In much of recent American fiction the hero is found to be reluctant to involve actively in the social process going on around him. He seems to be reduced just to a passive recipient of the bombardment of destructive elements of social experience. On the contrary, the Rothian hero wages a heroic struggle and confronts the nihilistic forces though the outcome may not be what he wished or intended. But his moral quest invariably begins and ends in the ambience of society and not in the abyss of loneliness. Tony Tanner pertinently remarks in this context: "It is perhaps an awareness of having this talent which made him feel that the contemporary novel should stress outer reality more and self less".[43] Roth firmly believes that any tenable solution of human problems is feasible through the mutual interaction of human beings because they are the ultimate source of all human virtues. Roth particularly liked the hero of Ellison's *Invisible Man* who fights his lonely battle though he finds himself utterly alone in the end. Roth praises his willing participation in the social process: "Not that he hasn't gone out into the world; he has gone out into it, and out into it, and out into it...."[44]

A majority of Roth's characters – Neil, Gabe, Paul, Tarnopol, Zuckerman and Kepesh – are distinct from the typical figure emerging from the recent American fiction in the absurdist mode in the sense that they are not swept off their feet by the deluge of postmodern destructive experience. Portnoy, who is immersed in sexual mire, is morbidly aware of his responsibility and moral duty to his family and society as a good Jewish boy. Even Sabbath, the "Destroyer of Morals", after wandering through the urban incoherence and chaos in his moral quest ultimately discovers his moorings in family and society.[45] McDaniel has convincingly argued that Roth is basically concerned with man in society and "his heroes must make their quest through the recognizable social world".[46] The subjects of his novels may be as diverse as baseball, masturbation, corrupt politicians and freakish intellectuals; his fictional background may be psychological, political or academic; through his experience in the diverse fields of postwar American social reality, Roth examines the human issues of perennial significance.

The Rothian protagonist, as stated earlier, cherishes and believes in the moral ideals based on humanitarian values and strives to achieve self-fulfillment. When his wishes and aspirations are not consummated he perceives the necessity to choose from the alternatives available to him. In making his choices he is guided mainly by his instinctive wisdom derived directly from the heart. When the specific course of action chosen by him does not lead to the resolution of his conflicts he feels the pangs of despair and frustration. Even so, he does not attempt to search for an escape route through social and moral vacuum. Notwithstanding his temporary failure, he again engages himself in the social and moral process with renewed vigor and courage. Eventually, he learns to make the necessary alterations in his response to the outer reality and achieves spiritual harmony and peace without compromising his individual values.

Neil in *Goodbye, Columbus* wants to achieve his love, Brenda, keeping intact, at the same time, his integrity and dignity. Brenda is expected by her parents to prove her loyalty to them which they feel they deserve owing to the material comforts provided to her by them. Her value system compels her to choose her parents while Neil prefers to preserve his identity and integrity. Gabe in *Letting Go* is caught inextricably in the web of interpersonal relationships despite his altruistic intentions. He has to choose between social involvement and preservation of his personal freedom. In *When She Was Good,* Lucy is bent upon proving the supremacy of her value system even in the face of fierce opposition from the dehumanizing forces of normalcy. Sometimes this conflict becomes internal within the soul of the protagonist who, like Doctor Faustus, painfully witnesses his fall unable to gather enough courage and strength to avert it. Portnoy in *Portnoy's Complaint* is torn by the painful conflict between moral responsibility and his urge to gratify his sexual desires. Similarly, David Kepesh in *The Professor of Desire* suffers the conflict between "reckless erotic ambitions and conscientious intellectual dedication".[47]

Significantly, none of the protagonists mentioned above succumbs under the tension of the adverse forces and withdraws in his lonely self away from his socially recognizable world like the protagonist of, for example, Fyodor Dostoevsky's *Notes from Underground,* Franz Kafka's "Metamorphosis", or Arthur Miller's *Death of a Salesman*. The intensity of the moral struggle of Roth's characters is heightened by their firm belief in the righteousness of their ethical pursuits. What Roth says about himself largely holds true in the case of his protagonists though they are certainly not his mouthpiece. He remarks in *Reading Myself and Others*: "Now I knew that no matter how hard I tried I could never really hope to be wicked...."[48] Roth's protagonists seem to be obsessed by a tendency to judge things through the perspective of their inherent morality. But when the moral assertion of a character crosses the limits, it turns into self-righteousness and ultimately proves destructive for the individual and the social system as well. Roth delineates his characters with keen moral sense but avoids proclaiming explicitly his approval or disapproval of them using the yardstick of his own moral preferences. He states in *Reading Myself and Others* that in his novels virtues and values are 'proposed' as they generally are in fiction – neither apart from the novel's predominant concern nor in perfect balance with it, but largely through the manner of presentation: through what might be called the sensuous aspects of fiction – tone, mood, voice, and, among other things, the juxtaposition of the narrative events themselves.[49]

It goes without saying that the Rothian protagonist is not able to resolve his conflicts suddenly and miraculously. He undergoes a gradual process of comprehending the nature of the conflicts and the moral alternatives available to him in the given circumstances. All his previous experiences leave deep impressions, and sometimes even lacerations, on his psyche and, in turn, brings about a substantial change in his outlook and behavior. He begins to comprehend the true nature of reality, vulnerability of his beliefs and the necessity of some modification in his behavior and attitude.

Each of the novels selected for this study demonstrates a definite stage in the development of the protagonist, which will be again modified by his future experience till a certain stability becomes manifest in the evolution of his ethical norms. In the first novel analyzed in this study, *Goodbye, Columbus,* the protagonist, Neil Klugman, confronts certain basic predicaments concerning his conduct in the world of personal relationships. After the failure of his love affair, he goes back to his work firmly convinced of the incompatibility of the consummation of his love and preservation of his integrity and selfhood. Right from the beginning of his love affair with Brenda, he is aware of the social and economic disparity between their circumstances; still, he is naive enough to believe that she would sacrifice her materialistic comforts for his sake. In the end, he realizes that the moral values he upholds are not recognized by the affluent suburban Patimkins who evaluate human relationships and happiness solely in terms of materialistic possessions. Nevertheless, instead of feeling victimized and estranged, he beats a retreat for introspection at the end of the novel.

In the next novel, *Letting Go,* the protagonist embarks upon his moral voyage to achieve self-fulfillment through interpersonal relationships. Under the literary influence of Henry James, Gabe Wallach is highly conscious of his lofty moral ideals and vows to do good to others. With his philanthropic intentions and motives, he involves himself in other people's affairs only to realize finally that complete personal freedom is inconsistent with interpersonal involvement. Ironically, his altruistic and generous gestures are met with rudeness and cruelty. His pursuit of moral goals is further hampered by his discovery of the inevitable encroachment made by the society upon his privacy. At the end of the novel, he sets on a tour of Europe for a temporary respite from the social entanglements.

The protagonist of *When She Was Good* is trapped inextricably in the web of small town normative morality. Here, Roth seems to bring out the consequences of egoism and self-righteousness. Initially, Lucy's resentment against and objection to the breach of family's code of conduct by her father is mild and, to some extent, justifiable. But in her self-righteousness, she completely ignores the demands of her family and community and stretches her moral principles to the extreme limits. Totally convinced of her moral superiority, she adamantly wants others to adhere to the ethical code envisaged by her and consequently ends up in schizophrenia and tragic death. In the later part of the novel, Roth makes more and more use of irony to bring into sharp focus Lucy's deviation from the broader and more humane value system upheld by Willard Carroll, and, perhaps, by her creator. Roth's commitment to a secular and universal morality is evidently clear in his objective and detached narrative and use of irony to suggest the fallibility of a character.

In *Portnoy's Complaint*, Roth explores his ethical concerns in a comic mode. Here, the protagonist is afflicted with both kinds of conflicts, external as well as internal. His desires for self-fulfillment are denied by his Jewish family and the larger Gentile society on the one hand, and by his guilt-ridden conscience on the other. Being morbidly conscious of his moral responsibility as a virtuous Jewish boy, he cannot rebel against his society and his family. Owing to his distorted vision, he discovers that sexuality is his only weapon against his family as well as the Gentile American society in which he feels alienated. As a young person, therefore, he wants to conquer America through sleeping with *shikshes*. Due to his moral rectitude, mainly rooted in his inherited Judaic value system, he finds himself inadequate to the demands of his family, society and his own conscience. In his opinion, his actions are grotesquely incongruous with his lofty moral ideals. In fact, Portnoy is at an advanced state of maturity than Neil, Gabe and Lucy inasmuch as he, after suffering the conflict between his inherent Jewish values and those of the secular society of America is able to comprehend more clearly the limitations of the former in the context of a broader universal morality. Inspite of his last howl of pain, the novel does not end pessimistically. After his sordid encounter with Naomi in Israel, he begins to understand his predicament and despite his fantastical self-abasement resolves to extricate himself from the maze of his narrow ethnicity and sexual obsessions. His visit to his doctor to get rid of his 'complaint' is in itself a sufficient evidence of his ethical progress and evolution.

The Professor of Desire is of crucial significance because here Roth brings together the diverse elements of moral struggle of the protagonist. Through complex human relationships, Roth delineates the individual's problem of choosing the moral alternatives available to him in the chaotic existential reality. David Kepesh feels the conflict between his sensual desires and his ethical impulses. With rare compassion and maturity, Roth depicts the struggle of a man to extricate himself from the mire of self-gratification. Shechner rightly calls it "a novel of convalescence".[50] In *The Professor of Desire,* the Rothian protagonist begins to understand his true nature and his place in the larger scheme of a supreme universal power. He feels the necessity of some modification in his response to the outer reality to ensure his survival as human entity without compromising his moral ideals. By exerting his maximum strength, he sublimates his baser instincts into higher moral virtues and resolves his conflict attaining thereby spiritual harmony and integration of personality. Though his happiness and peace is tentative like all other things in life, it is by no means a small achievement for a common human being.

As mentioned earlier, Roth feels that the contemporary writer finds it difficult to "understand, describe, and then make credible much of American reality."[51] In order to express the social reality, he has evolved a highly flexible fictional style. Through the skilful manipulation of his language and his narrative techniques, he has been able to express effectively the complex response of the modern man to existential reality. Though most of his protagonists are intellectual and sophisticated urban people, he has convincingly and realistically portrayed a great variety of characters from different spheres of life. He has achieved this remarkable feat mainly through his flair for the colloquial and vernacular language. The apparent naturalness and spontaneity of his prose is the result of his skilful maneuvering of syntax and diction.

Similarly, his experiments with various narrative techniques to provide exact form and shape to his fictional material have been acclaimed by most critics. Though his most favored narrative technique seems to be the first person point of view, which he employs in the majority of his novels, he has successfully used other modes of narration suited to his artistic purpose. In *Zuckerman Unbound, The Anatomy Lesson, Sabbath's Theater* and some of his short stories, he unfolds his plot through third person omniscient point of view. But he can modulate his narrative technique with virtuosity depending upon the demand of the particular occasion or character. For example, he has made partial use of omniscient third person point of view in *Letting Go, When She Was Good and My Life as a Man*. For his most popular protagonist, Portnoy, Roth devises a new confessional strategy, "the psychoanalytic monologue," perfectly suited to his peculiar moral and psychological dilemma.[52] His experimentation sometimes becomes intricate and confusing as in the novels *The Counterlife* and *Deception* where he employs multiple points of view to filter the fictional experience through various centers of consciousness leaving it, finally, to the reader to interpret it in his own way. This may partly be ascribed to the complex nature of his fictional material which tends to defy an exact definition and presentation through the conventional modes of narration.

For my purpose, I have selected only five of his novels for detailed study, which are from his earlier work. They include *Goodbye, Columbus, Letting Go, When She Was Good, Portnoy's Complaint* and *The Professor of Desire*. The reasons for this selection are many. For one thing, Roth is such a voluminous writer that it is not feasible to study in detail all his novels. He has published more than twenty novels so far besides a number of short stories and his autobiography. The novels selected here are generally considered among his most significant ones from the point of view of his artistic achievement. Moreover, they were written during the early phase of his literary career when he was most intensely preoccupied with social and ethical aspects of human life. In his later novels, he explores still newer aspects of human experience through different themes and techniques. Taken together, these novels have a certain thematic unity and continuity and illustrates best the evolution of Roth's artistic genius. The book critically evaluates the response of the individual in Roth's fiction to the adverse outer and inner forces and the ethical choices made by him in the process of resolution of his conflicts.

REFERENCES

1. Malcolm Bradbury, *The Modern American Novel* (Oxford: Oxford UP, 1983), 131.
2. Tony Tanner, *City of Words: American Fiction 1950-1970* (New York: Harper, 1971), 18.
3. Philip Roth, *Reading Myself and Others* (New York: Farrar, 1975), 120.
4. Ihab Hassan, *Radical Innocence: Studies in the Contemporary American Novel* (Princeton: Princeton UP, 1961), 31.
5. Hassan 31.

6. John N. McDaniel, *The Fiction of Philip Roth* (Haddonfield, NJ: Haddonfield, 1974), 40.
7. Hassan 31.
8. Walter Allen, introduction, *The Modern Novel in Britain and the United States* (New York: Dutton, 1964), XV.
9. Mark Shechner, "Jewish Writers", *Harvard Guide to Contemporary American Writing*, ed. Daniel Hoffman (Delhi: Oxford UP, 1981), 198.
10. Ruth Wisse, *The Schlemiel as Modern Hero* (Chicago: U of Chicago P, 1971), 82.
11. Jeremy Larner, "The Conversion of the Jews", *Partisan Review* 27 (Fall 1960): 761.
12. Irving Howe, "Philip Roth Reconsidered", *Commentary* (Dec. 1972). Rpt. in *Critical Essays on Philip Roth*, ed. Sanford Pinsker (Boston: Hall, 1982), 230.
13. Theodore Solotaroff, "Philip Roth and the Jewish Moralists", *Chicago Review* 13 (Winter, 1959). Rpt. in *Contemporary American – Jewish Literature: Critical Essays*, ed. Irving Malin (Bloomington: Indiana UP, 1973), 15-16.
14. Roth, *Reading Myself* 150.
15. Roth, *Reading Myself* 152.
16. Roth, *Reading Myself* 20.
17. Shechner 232.
18. McDaniel 202.
19. McDaniel 40.
20. Tanner 313.
21. Judith Paterson Jones and Guinevera A. Nance, *Philip Roth* (New York: Ungar, 1981), 161.
22. Jones and Nance 162.
23. Hermione Lee, *Philip Roth* (London: Methuen, 1982), 83.
24. Shechner 232.

25. Shechner 220.

26. Shechner 236.

27. Searles 3.

28. Allen Guttmann, *The Jewish Writer in America: Assimilation and the Crisis of Identity* (New York: Oxford UP, 1971), 73.

29. Murray Baumgarten and Barbara Gottfried, *Understanding Philip Roth* (South Carolina: U of South Carolina P, 1990), 18.

30. Jay L. Halio, *Philip Roth Revisited* (New York: Twayne, 1992), 1.

31. Mary Allen,"When She Was Good She Was Horrid", *The Necessary Blankness: Women in Major American Fiction of the Sixties* (Urbana: U of Illinois P, 1976). Rpt. in Philip Roth, ed. Harold Bloom (New York: Chelsea, 1986), 146.

32. Mary Allen 146.

33. Hassan 31.

34. Saul Bellow, *Seize the Day* (London: Penguin, 1988), 118.

35. Bradbury 142-43.

36. Roth, *Reading Myself* 27.

37. Roth, *Reading Myself* 28.

38. Jones and Nance 7.

39. Lionel Trilling, *The Liberal Imagination* (Garden City, NY: Doubleday, 1953), 213.

40. Roth, *Reading Myself* 77.

41. McDaniel 206-07.

42. Roth, *Reading Myself* 53.

43. Tanner 312.

44. Roth, *Reading Myself* 135.

45. Roth, *Sabbath's Theater* (Boston: Houghton, 1995), 376.

46. McDaniel 49.

47. Lee 65.
48. Roth, *Reading Myself* 87.
49. Roth, *Reading Myself* 27.
50. Shechner 235.
51. Roth, Reading Myself 120.
52. Roth, Reading Myself 41.

2

High Idealism : *Goodbye, Columbus*

Goodbye, Columbus and Five Short Stories, published in 1959, was the first book written by Philip Roth and it won him the 1960 National Book Award for Fiction. The book, including *Goodbye, Columbus* and some other short stories was acclaimed widely as a serious work of fiction testifying to the earnest artistic purpose of a young and ambitious novelist. Some of the stories ("The Conversion of the Jews", "Defender of the Faith" and "Eli, the Fanatic") evoked an unfavorable reaction among the critics and the Rabbis owing to some controversial reference to the Jewish culture and tradition.

The novella *Goodbye, Columbus* is the most interesting and popular of all the stories contained in the book. It narrates the tale of a brief love affair between Neil Klugman, a young man from Newark, and Brenda Patimkin, a rich and pampered suburban girl from an affluent Jewish family. In his attempt to cross the social and economic boundaries for the purpose of the consummation of his love, Neil faces the clash of his value system with that upheld by the affluent Patimkins. When he is at close quarters with them, he discovers the moral barrenness under the glittering facade. Neil is a novice and idealistic initiate who is equally confused by the spiritually hollow life of the successful suburban Jews and the inherent value system of a "nice Jewish boy" who is never oblivious of his roots in Newark.[1] The affluent world of Short Hills, no doubt, fascinates him to begin with, but his experiences with Patimkins and their shallow value system cause such intense repulsion and moral indignation that Neil prefers to withdraw unobtrusively into his Newark ghetto life. In order to preserve his moral integrity and identity, he ultimately chooses to sacrifice his love. Brenda has naturally inherited and represents these false values. She has her full share of carnal pleasures and enjoyments to which she is accustomed and myopically – she is myopic literally – thinks that she has a legitimate and moral right to do so. From the very beginning she is shown to be a "practical girl".[2] Jay L. Halio pertinently remarks: "She knows her attractions, and she knows how to use them."[3] The choice between her rich parents at Short Hills and the poor librarian from Newark to her is rather simple and easy. She prefers to wallow in the comforts and luxuries provided by her parents leaving, inadvertently, permanent lacerations on Neil's psyche.

But the superficial simplicity of the story is deceptive, hiding underneath the complex social and moral issues. Judith Paterson Jones and Guinevera A. Nance find the narrative permeated by "the summer-romance theme and the vacation atmosphere."[4] On the other hand, Sanford Pinsker is of the opinion that despite the apparent theme of love the novella's "real concerns are socio-economic rather than erotic."[5] In *Goodbye, Columbus*, Roth explores the ethical instincts and motivations of the protagonist with rare earnestness and intensity. Neil does not seem to have any preconceived designs in making his advances towards Brenda. He falls headlong in love with her as is evidently clear in the first few pages of the novella. His feelings of love are genuine and sincere. It will perhaps be preposterous to suppose that Neil is trying to win Brenda with the ulterior motives of crossing "the hundred and eighty feet that the suburbs rose in altitude above Newark" (8). The love affair begins suddenly, unexpectedly and spontaneously :

> The first time I saw Brenda she asked me to hold her glasses. Then she stepped out to the edge of the diving board and looked foggily into the pool; it could have been drained, myopic Brenda would never have known it. ... I watched her move off. Her hands suddenly appeared behind her. She caught the bottom of her suit between thumb and index finger and flicked what flesh had been showing back where it belonged. My blood jumped.
>
> That night, before dinner, I called her. (3)

Obviously, prior to his arrival in the dreamland of Short Hills Neil's sole obsession is his love. But once in Short Hills, he is overawed by the "Horn of Plenty" in this world of materialistic luxury and abundance.[6] The suburb, with cool climate, sprawling lawns, sporting goods and refrigerators full of fresh fruits is in sharp contrast to the hot, congested, and poor Newark of Aunt Gladys. It seems as if the inhabitants of Short Hills refuse "to share the very texture of life with those of us outside" (8). He knows that he is an outsider in Short Hills, but in order to experience fulfillment of his love he sleeps with her in her own house. It is noteworthy that Brenda savors the sensual part of their love more greedily as she is more inclined to hedonistic pleasures. For Neil the sexual part is a complementary act for the consummation of their love while for Brenda the pleasure derived from the sexual act itself is the sole objective. In fact, sexual indulgence and moral guilt is a recurrent theme in Roth's fiction. Some of his later heroes like Portnoy and David Kepesh also indulge in sexual gratifications but with the difference that they have to suffer horribly the pangs of guilt owing to their inherent ethical values. Brenda does not seem to be guarded by any such ethical barrier and is driven solely by her sensual instincts.

Neil has been criticized by different critics as a clever Jew aspiring to the wealth of the Patimkins. Bernard F. Rodgers, Jr. tries to convince us that he is a crafty and manipulative young man strategically trying to win Brenda to fulfill his dream of success. According to him, if the *u* in Klugman is pronounced long rather than short in Yiddish, it means "clever fellow."[7] But it seems a far-fetched assumption. The name 'Neil Klugman' has been twisted by critics to connote a number of meanings. John N. McDaniel interprets the word as meaning "sadfellow" bringing to mind "the cry of the Jewish immigrant, cursing the unkept promises of the new world."[8] Though Neil cherishes the dream of success and, during his stay in Short Hills, occasionally assumes the role of the inheritor of Ben Patimkin's wealth, his sole objective, however, is the consummation of his love on ethical terms. Actually, his postponement of the marriage proposal to Brenda may be partly due to his disappointment at the absence of his cherished ethical values in the world of Brenda and her family.

Jones and Nance, comparing Neil to T.S. Eliot's Prufrock in his hesitation and inaction, point out that he is in "a kind of limbo"[9] drifting "through his love affair and his job with the same lack of commitment to permanency."[10] To understand his confusion and dilemma it is necessary to see his love for Brenda and his romantic dream of an affluent life in different perspectives. His love for Brenda is genuine, sincere and not qualified by any overt or covert condition. On some occasions he is obsessed with her idea to such a degree that he avoids even Aunt Gladys whom he adores. In such moments he "didn't care for anything but Brenda"(16-17).

At the same time like the hero in contemporary American fiction, he wishes to rise socially and economically. Though this is not an obsession in his case, its presence cannot be denied. But it is preposterous to link this element of ambition with his ultimate search for higher ethical values.

The conflict in Neil's mind is two-fold. Initially, his romantic idealism is seen to be in clash with the superficial way of life in Short Hills. Later on, he gradually comes to comprehend the truth of the pampered and irresponsible personality of Brenda herself. But in the meantime his emotional attachment with her has grown so deep that he finds it difficult to disengage himself. After the dream sequence where he along with the Negro boy waves adieu to the native women, it is amply clear that his love is doomed to failure. When Brenda manages to extend his stay in her house for another week he reflects :

> This should have made me overjoyed, but ... I was not joyful but disturbed, as I had been more and more with the thought that when Brenda went back to Radcliffe, that would be the end for me. I was convinced that even Miss Winney's stool was not high enough for me to see clear up to Boston. Nevertheless, I tossed my clothing back into the drawer and was able, finally, to tell myself that there'd been no hints of ending our affair from Brenda, and any suspicions I had, any uneasiness, was spawned in my own uncertain heart." (75-76)

Yet, he obsessively runs after Brenda only to confront the reality of her love in the hotel room when she categorically and unambiguously declares her choice to desert him in favor of her parents and the comfortable life they can buy for her. At this crucial juncture he has to make his final choice. Instead of pursuing dream-like Brenda he prefers to preserve his selfhood and identity.

Neil, like Gabe Wallach, Peter Tarnopol, Nathan Zuckerman and David Kepesh is an intellectual and sensitive young man, highly conscious of his moral responsibilities. Though he has been a student of philosophy his motives are almost invariably guided by his heart-felt instincts instead of logic. He falls in love with Brenda instinctively and, significantly enough, before he has a real glimpse of the dazzling life of Short Hills. He is swept off his feet by its prosperity and luxury so glaringly in contrast with the gloomy Newark of Aunt Gladys :

> I opened the door of the old refrigerator; it was not empty. No longer did it hold butter, eggs, herring in cream sauce, ginger ale, tuna fish salad, an occasional corsage – rather it was heaped with fruit, shelves swelled with it, every color, every texture, and hidden within, every kind of pit. There were greengage plums, black plums, red plums, apricots, nectarines, peaches, long horns of grapes, black, yellow, red, and cherries, cherries flowing out of boxes and staining everything scarlet. And there were melons – cantaloupes and honeydews – and on the top shelf, half of a huge watermelon, a thin sheet of wax paper clinging to its bare red face like a wet lip. Oh Patimkin! Fruit grew in their refrigerator and sporting goods dropped from their trees! (43)

But before long he realizes the vacuity and meaninglessness of their life. He comes face to face with the moral and spiritual degeneration of American *nouveaux riches*. Brenda turns out to be a spoiled and lazy girl who does not know "what a day's work means" (64). She is always found playing games, eating or enjoying sexual pleasures with Neil. Julie, the younger sister, always wants to win without any effort and hates Neil when he deliberately defeats her. Instantly, she turns malicious and accuses him venomously: "You cheat! And you were stealing fruit!"(45). Her brother, Ronald, totally unaware of the hard and painful realities of a less fortunate life, lives complacently on material comforts provided by his father. Not surprisingly, Mr. Patimkin and his wife, proud of their ascent to the suburban Short Hills from the Jewish Ghetto of Newark, evaluate every human value in terms of money. Mr.Patimkin writes in his letter to Brenda, "I love you honey if you want a coat I'll buy You a coat" (127). The Patimkins have replaced the humanistic values of love, charity and generosity with shallow and vulgar display of wealth.

In the suburban Short Hills, Neil is so acutely and painfully conscious of the difference in social and economic status of the Patimkins and his own that he sometimes feels a dualism in his motives regarding his love for Brenda. He feels "suddenly angry" when Brenda tells him that they lived in Newark "when I [she] was a baby" (12). Thus, the rich suburban life of the Patimkins is, paradoxical though it may seem, a hindrance in the consummation of his love. Later, when Brenda again refers to Newark, Neil thinks that he "did not want to voice a word that would lift the cover and reveal that hideous emotion I always felt for her, and is the underside of love"(27). This "hideous emotion" is related to his dislike of all the hypocrisy, artificiality and lack of emotional depth which she has in her personality. The fact that the Patimkins were the inhabitants of Newark before their dream of success came true stirs that chord in his heart which ties him to Brenda. Though the Newarkian milieu is not depicted in detail in the novella, its presence is always hovering in the mind of Neil. That is why some critics think that the story is about the "class conflict" between the "have-nots of Newark" and "the haves of Short Hills."[11] The fact which is generally overlooked is that Brenda has imbibed all the shallow and superficial values from her family about which Neil comes to know gradually through his intimacy with her in her own house.

Brenda does not seem to have the slightest exposure to the cruelty and suffering of the world outside her orbit of complacency and comforts. That she is more a fairy than an earthly being is suggested in the imagery used by the author in his description of her personality. When Neil kisses her for the first time he feels a "fluttering of wings – tiny wings no bigger than her breasts"(14). She is unable to see beyond her hedonistic and carnal desires and their fulfillment. She can deceive and manipulate her parents when it suits her purpose. In this respect, she seems to be a precursor of some later heroines of Roth, like Mary Jane Reed, Sharon Shatsky, and Birgitta Svanstromi who obsessively hanker after sexual pleasures. She is more interested in Neil's body than any other virtue in his personality. Her philosophy of love is reflected on the occasion when she asks Neil whether he loves her. When he does not give any answer she says, "I'll sleep with you whether you do or not, so tell me the truth" (51). Neil is naturally surprised that she has not "asked me anything about me" (18). She is only interested in the pursuit of her sensual gratification. There is also a hint of her flirtation with Luther Ferrari "whom Brenda had dated for a whole year in high school" (55). After her quarrel with her mother she takes Neil to a room in her house and frantically searches for the money her father had hidden for her for a rainy day. Her animal instincts are suggested in her posture: "She was on her hands and knees in front of the sofa and was holding up its paunch to peek beneath" (67). Unable to find the money there, "among the disarrangement and dirt" she at once directs Neil to make love to her there and then and Neil obeys her (68). This episode amply demonstrates her moral vacuity, which manifests itself in either materialistic acquisition or sexual gratification. The imagery and diction employed by the author strongly evokes the image of Kurtz, the protagonist of Joseph Conrad's *Heart of Darkness*, who is seen "crawling on all fours" in the wilderness of Africa for materialistic acquisition.[12]

Quite naturally, the choice for Brenda is clear after the discovery of the diaphragm by her mother. Neil accuses her of leaving it in her room intentionally to break off their relation while she pleads that she left it there just by chance. But whether she put it there deliberately or by chance is beside the point. Whereas Neil is ready to accept her without the social and economic status attached to the Patimkins, the thought of choosing him at the expense of her family is totally unacceptable to her. Thus, it is evidently clear that given her family background and frivolous nature she is least likely to feel any pangs of remorse and guilt while deserting him.

But the dilemma in Neil's mind is more complex. That the love affair with Brenda is doomed to failure dawns upon him as early as the opening lines of section six of the novella. But his firm faith in his love still moves him forward. He is susceptible more to the exhortations of his heart than to the calculations of his mind. He naively hopes for those values in Brenda which she sadly lacks and the poignant realization of this fact makes him more wretched. After the affair is over he ruminates: "If she had only been slightly *not* Brenda ... but then would I have loved her?"(136). What he does not realize at this initial stage of his ethical quest is that Brenda is an epitome of those false values which form an integral part of contemporary American society. Sometimes he sees himself in the role of Mr.Patimkin's son-in-law and partner in his wealth. When he goes to Mr. Patimkin's office to fetch some silver patterns for Mrs. Patimkin, he toys with this idea: "Suddenly I could see myself directing the Negroes – I would have an ulcer in an hour"(91-92). For one thing, such scenes are comic in nature. Secondly, whenever he visualizes himself as part of the Patimkins he feels doubtful of the compatibility of the satiety of his acquisitive self with his determination to keep intact his moral integrity. In his initiation into the social and moral experience, Neil is similar to such American heroes as Twain's Huck Finn, Melville's Ahab, Fitzgerald's Gatsby and Hemingway's Nick Adams. His confrontation with social reality assumes that "form of initiation", to use Hassan's words, the end of which is "confirmation."[13] The protagonist in *Goodbye, Columbus* is at the initial stage of his ethical evolution. After disengaging himself from his messy love relationship he would have gained valuable insight into social reality and his own motives.

Neil's disillusionment with the American social reality is juxtaposed with the dehumanization of Leo Patimkin – the half brother of Ben Patimkin – who is among the guests on the occasion of Ronald's wedding. It is not without purpose that Roth makes Neil, of all the guests present there, to hear the long discourse of Leo, a typical Jewish failure like Bellow's Tommy Wilhelm. Like Willy Loman of Arthur Miller's *Death of a Salesman* he is a salesman and travels long distances to sell bulbs. He represents the cosmopolitan Jew ever exploring new fields and opportunities: "For the world was Leo's territory, every city, ever swamp, every road and highway (118). He is an embodiment of the shattered dreams and thwarted desires of modern man in materialistic American society. His poverty and helplessness is in sharp contrast with the vulgar display of newly acquired wealth by the Patimkins at Ronald's wedding. Under the soothing effect of champagne he confesses to Neil: "Everything good in my life I can count on my fingers!" (116) His strange kinship with Neil derives partly from the innate sadness of not belonging to the charming social circle of Short Hills. However, Halio's attempt to trace the figure of a *schlemiel* in Neil does not seem to be justified, as Neil is too sophisticated and sober to fit such a figure (14). Through the figure of Leo, Roth brings into sharp focus Neil's disinclination to be a passive victim like the former. He seems to suggest Neil's firm commitment to his ethical values despite the temptation and demands of his circumstances. Leo, on the other hand, displays all the attributes of a *schlemiel*. He is victimized by his circumstances, yet he manages to survive in his society with his antics.

A more striking parallel of Neil is to be found in the Negro boy who visits the Newark Public Library frequently to look at the Gauguin paintings. "Man, that's the fuckin life", he exclaims in euphoria, watching the exotic paintings of native women of Tahiti island (37). The beautiful life painted in the book is out of reach of the Negro boy and the Short Hills suburban life is a distant dream for Neil. Both are denied the materialization of their dream of a rich life. Later, Neil's ruminations reflect a similar sense of surprise and awe at the splendor of Short Hills which he "could see now, in my mind's eye, at dusk, rose-colored, like a Gauguin stream" (38). Pinsker thinks that the Negro boy is an alter ego of Neil. Pinsker further observes, "Also, his alternating bravado and uneasiness at the library is a mirror image of Klugman's own behavior in the alien ground of Short Hills."[15] Moreover, Neil recognizes his identification with the boy by securing for him the book even at the risk of offending other readers. Again, their identification is reinforced in the dream scene where the boat carrying them is moving away from the seashore. The Negro boy accuses him for this disaster while Neil tells him that it was his fault because he did not have a library card. But definitely they were moving "further and further from the island" which symbolizes their lost paradise (75).

In his books, Roth has delineated parents-children relationship in all its intricacy and complexity. At one end of the ethical spectrum is the tender, affectionate and dutiful son in *Patrimony*, while at the other end is Lucy

Nelson, the heroine of *When She Was Good,* with her burning hatred and disgust for her father. In *Goodbye, Columbus,* Neil's parents are represented by Aunt Gladys who is a virtuous, hardworking and responsible lady. Though she has not much role in the narrative, she is an epitome of humanitarian virtues. Halio rightly remarks that "she is not merely a figure of fun but a standard of humanity" against which other characters lose their lusture.[16] She is a stereotypical Jewish mother figure though she lacks the possessiveness and overprotectiveness of Sophie Portnoy of *Portnoy's Complaint*. Neil is tender and affectionate to her even though he has a tendency to be wary of her parental authority and carefully avoids any encroachment upon his personal freedom.

Conversely, in the case of the Patimkins money seems to be the criterion through which all human relations are evaluated. Brenda loves her parents (particularly her doting father) and owes them her unqualified loyalty because of the material goods she receives from them. Not surprisingly, she sometimes nurses bitter feelings towards her mother because her stern attitude poses a barrier in the fulfillment of her wayward desires. In exchange for the comfortable life provided to their children, Mr.Patimkin and his wife demand a particular kind of conduct from them. They are naturally disturbed when they learn about the sexual intimacy between their daughter and Neil. Mrs. Patimkin writes in her letter: "But you drifted away from your family, even though we sent you to the best schools and gave you the best money could buy" (129). Similar is the case with Julie and Ronald, who are the typical product of the affluent upper class American society. Roth painstakingly depicts the family life of the Patimkins to imply that his protagonists embark upon their quest for their identity from the ambience of the oldest social institution devised by mankind. In this respect Roth is certainly distinct from many of his contemporaries whose heroes act in the orbit of their loneliness. For Roth, family relationships are pivotal for affirmation and verification of individual moral values. But it must be admitted that the canvas of *Goodbye, Columbus* is too small to allow the portrayal of the intricacies of familial relations in detail as found in such later novels as *Letting Go, When She Was Good, Portnoy's Complaint* and *The Professor of Desire*.

Various critics have pointed out a disturbing lack of commitment in Neil's character. For example, Ben Siegel points out that Neil is "determinedly uncommitted" towards his surroundings and his "lack of purpose prevents his accepting, rejecting or defining either his Jewishness or his social role."[17] Similarly, Jones and Nance remark that due to his "incapacity for commitment", Neil goes on procrastinating his marriage proposal to Brenda.[18] This seems to be a flaw in his character that he has no concrete idea regarding his future course of action. He himself admits frankly that he is not a "planner" (51) though he is certain that the "library was not going to be my lifework" (32). His love affair does not seem to be guided by any preconceived and ulterior motive other than his instincts. The romance which began so spontaneously eventually leads to his sharp realization of the need for preservation of his identity in spiritually barren and affluent world of Short Hills. Neil is morbidly aware of the ghetto life in Newark awaiting him after the summer vacations. But despite a seeming non-seriousness of purpose on his part there is no apparent indication of the possibility of his compromise with his innate moral values, howsoever fascinating the suburban dream may be.

Neil's commitment to his intrinsic value system sometimes manifests itself in the form of mild outburst of anger and indignation at the most trivial hint of moral blemish on him. In the dream sequence when the boat is moving away from the seashore the Negro boy "shouted at me that it was my fault and I shouted it was his for not having a library card"(74). In Brenda's house he sometimes "felt like Carlota [the maid-servant]; no, not even as comfortable as that"(40). Similarly, when Julie displays some misgivings about his eating the fruit from their refrigerator he mercilessly defeats her as if to take revenge. Whether with his colleagues in the library or with the Patimkins in Short Hills, he steadfastly adheres to his moral values and is not willing to conform to the forces of normalcy. Seen in this context, the affluence of the Patimkins turns out to be a hindrance in the fulfillment of his love. Therefore, in his own heart the conflicting instincts – his love for Brenda and his dream of success – seem to overlap.

Later in the novel, instead of making his marriage proposal Neil asks Brenda to get a diaphragm. Initially, she shows her reluctance to use the device, yet finally on his insistence she agrees. Unfortunately, it is discovered by her mother in her room. Though Neil has a foreboding of the failure of their love relation when Brenda manipulates to extend his stay in their house for another week, the shock comes with full force in their last meeting in the hotel room. Brenda shows him her parents' letters which leave no doubt about the hypocrisy of their value system. Mr. Patimkin's reaction, though mild and enwrapped in a somewhat false assurance of freedom to his children, clearly and unambiguously conveys the message that Brenda should have nothing to do with Neil in future: "As for your mistake it takes Two to make a mistake and now that you will be away at school and from him and what you got involved in you will probably do all right I have every faith you will" (127). As for Mrs.Patimkin's letter, it is more sarcastic and malicious as she does not approve of Brenda's wayward and irresponsible behavior from the very beginning. She candidly gives vent to her sense of shock and disbelief on such horrid conduct of her daughter as well as Neil: "That the two of you should be carrying on like that in our very house I will never in my life be able to understand"(129). Particularly in the matter of money and sexual conduct her mother's response derives from the remnants of a Jewish value system inherited from her old Newark background.

In the hotel room, the interchange between Neil and Brenda brings into sharp focus the choices each has to make at this crucial juncture of their love affair. Neil's accusation that Brenda deliberately left the diaphragm in his room brings to surface his subconscious apprehensions regarding her preferences for a luxurious life. Almost convinced of the failure of their love relation, Neil directly throws the question to Brenda. The following interchange of words clearly brings out their conflicts and priorities:

"Neil, be realistic. After this, can I bring you home? Can you see us all sitting around the table?"

"I can't if you can't, and I can if you can".

"Are you going to speak Zen, for God's sake!"

"Brenda, the choices aren't mine. You can bring Linda or me. You can go home or not go home. That's another choice. Then you don't even have to worry about choosing between me and Linda."

"Neil, you don't understand. They are still my parents. They did send me to the best schools, didn't they? They have given me everything I've wanted, haven't they?"(133-34).

Neil is ready to accept Brenda if only she reciprocates his love irrespective of her social and economic status. If Neil had been clever and crafty and had any intentions to use her, he certainly would have tried to persuade and manipulate her. He is prepared to face his ultimate fate, which he has been apprehending probably for a long time. It might appear that lack of a determined pursuit of his love is the reason of his postponement of his marriage proposal to Brenda till it is too late. But it is his idealism that prevents him to cultivate those pragmatic traits in his character which are necessary for survival in the upper class society of Short Hills. In contrast, Brenda is not troubled by any ethical dilemma in her mind regarding the choice between Neil and her parents. She chooses her parents who are capable of providing her the necessary security and material well-being in life.

Regarding the termination of the love affair there are different versions offered by different critics. McDaniel observes: "In rejecting Brenda, he has lost a dream and gained a sad insight into the shallowness of his quest."[19] He has realized the futility of Mr.Patimkin's wealth in attaining spiritual harmony and prepares to embark upon his moral quest with renewed vigor and determination. Rodgers is of the opinion that Neil's plans to grab Mr. Patimkin's riches through Brenda have "backfired."[20] And it is she who has rejected him and not vice versa. This line of contention appears flawed. Brenda apparently rejects him in favor of her parents on the occasion of their last meeting in the hotel room. But prior to her decision, Neil clearly demonstrates his utter disgust with the value system she and her family have chosen.

Standing in front of the Lamont Library (which, ironically, "had Patimkin Sinks in its rest rooms")(135), Neil tries to analyze the failure of his love affair:

> I simply looked at myself in the mirror the light made of the window. I was only that substance, I thought, those limbs, that face that I saw in front of me. I looked, but the outside of me gave up little information about the inside of me. ... What was it inside me that had turned pursuit and clutching into love, and then turned it inside out again? What was it

that had turned winning into losing, and losing – who knows – into winning? I was sure I had loved Brenda, though standing there, I knew I couldn't any longer. And I knew it would be a long while before I made love to anyone the way I had made love to her (135-36).

Initially, Neil was not able to visualize in their true perspectives the two most forceful motives in his heart – love for Brenda and his dream of a high social and economic life. It appears that now he has gained an insight into the gap between his apparent engagement in frivolous pursuits and the reality of his inner moral being. His deeply ingrained idealistic values come in the way of his winning his love. Though he has lost Brenda, he has kept intact his selfhood and moral identity which were at stake in his pursuit of Brenda. He neither compromises his values nor succumbs to any acquisitive temptations in his spiritual quest. This is his ethical triumph and it promises him an assurance of self-realization and the possibilities of survival as a human entity in the contemporary reality.

REFERENCES

1. Philip Roth, *Reading Myself and Others* (New York: Farrar, 1975) 37.
2. Roth, *Goodbye, Columbus and Five Short Stories*, 30th Anniversary ed. (Boston: Houghton, 1989) 7. All subsequent citations will be to the text as given in this edition and the page numbers will be indicated in parentheses appearing immediately after the quotation.
3. Jay L. Halio, *Philip Roth Revisited* (New York: Twayne, 1992) 21.
4. Judith Paterson Jones and Guinevera A Nance, *Philip Roth* (New York: Ungar, 1981) 13.
5. Sanford Pinsker, *The Comedy That 'Hoits': An Essay on the Fiction of Philip Roth* (Columbia: U of Missouri P, 1975) 5.
6. W.B. Yeats, "A Prayer for My Daughter", *W.B. Yeasts:*

Selected Poetry, ed. A. Norman Jeffares (London: Pan, 1974) 101.

7. Bernard F. Rodgers, Jr., *Philip Roth* (Boston: Twayne, 1978) 45.
8. John N. McDaniel, *The Fiction of Philip Roth* (Haddonfield, NJ: Haddonfield, 1974) 74.
9. Jones and Nance 16.
10. Jones and Nance 13.
11. Pinsker 7.
12. Joseph Conrad, *Heart of Darkness* (Harmondsworth: Penguin, 1974) 93.
13. Ahab Hassan, *Radical Innocence: Studies in the Contemporary American Novel* (Princeton: Princeton UP, 1961) 35.
14. Halio 15.
15. Pinsker 10.
16. Halio 21.
17. Ben Siegel, "Jewish Fiction and the Affluent Society", *Northwest Review* 4 (Spring 1961): 91.
18. Jones and Nance 13.
19. McDaniel 74.
20. Rodgers 42.

3

The Engulfing Chaos : *Letting Go*

Letting Go, the first full-length novel of Roth, was published in 1962. It is similar to *Goodbye, Columbus* and Roth's other novels in its basic concerns of moral implications of individual existence in family and society, and the resultant conflicts and their resolution. But here the canvas is larger and the young novelist explores human relationships in all their intricacies and complexities. The novel evoked a mixed response; some critics hailed it as a great novel in the manner of Henry James, the unequalled master of human motives and conscience, while others regarded it as a 'mistake'.[1] But now when the critical opinion regarding Roth's fiction is well-established, it has generally been agreed that *Letting Go* is a serious novel in the tradition of Henry James and Leo Tolstoy, who, at that time, had a profound influence on Roth. Technically also, Roth amply demonstrates his skills in manipulating various narrative techniques to handle his fictional material. The major part of the novel is written from first person point of view where Gabe Wallach, the protagonist, is the narrator while in some sections third person narrator is employed to explore the psyche of other major characters.

Earlier many critics thought it to be a tiring, tedious and gloomy book which chronicles several years in the lives of five confused and unhappy people. Mark Shechner, for example, complained of "gray and depressive background" of the novel.[2] *Letting Go*, however, should be viewed in the background of the fifties when the young graduates tended to assume serious and responsible airs and prove their adulthood. And besides, the largest part of the novel is set in Chicago where Roth himself was a graduate student and later a part-time faculty member in the university. The novel is a remarkable study of human motives, interpersonal relationships and moral dilemmas. It delineates with rare profundity the predicament of modern man caught in the web of moral obligations and personal aspirations. *Letting Go*, according to Judith Paterson Jones and Guinevera A. Nance "anticipates Roth's next two novels, *When She Was Good* and *Portnoy's Complaint*, not only in its emphasis on the family as a particularly powerful force but also in its ironic examination of the idea of being or doing 'good'."[3] Roth is preoccupied here with such serious issues as individual desires, manipulation of others for selfish purpose, need for privacy, and feelings of responsibility and guilt. In *Letting Go*, as in all Roth's fiction, the protagonist's search for self-fulfillment passes through the maze of familial and social relationships.

In *Letting Go* the hero involves himself thoroughly in interpersonal relationships to achieve his objectives. George J. Searles rightly points out: "*Letting Go* seems to suggest that conflict is inevitable in close interpersonal relationships and that human dealings are intrinsically and unavoidably enigmatic, especially within the family circle."[4] Through the two main characters, Gabe Wallach and Paul Herz, Roth traces the painful struggle of the individual to achieve manhood and maturity in contemporary American society. Bernard F. Rodgers, Jr. is of the opinion that Paul is Gabe's opposite in many ways.

Outwardly, at least, they are presented in contrasting ways. Whereas Gabe is financially secure and burdened with comparatively less responsibilities except, perhaps, his lonely widower father, Paul from the very beginning is seen to be overburdened with poverty and his obligations to his parents and wife. Their reaction to the suppressive and intrusive outward forces is also different; Paul tolerates them with a rare kind of stoicism and fortitude while Gabe shows a tendency to feel embarrassed and impatient at the slightest hint of violation of his privacy.

The title of the first section "Debts and Sorrows" is important in its suggestion of the basic themes of the novel. Rodgers points out the significance of the title :

> "'Debts' conveys the nature of the troublesome moral choices, complicated by the conflict between duty and personal desires for self-satisfaction, which weigh heavily on the consciences of each of the novel's major characters."[5]

Significantly, the novel opens with the letter of Gabe's mother from her death-bed and it sets the tone of the novel. She confesses that her desire to do good to others throughout her life had been the cause of much unhappiness to others :

> *Since I was a little girl I always wanted to be Very Decent to People. Other little girls wanted to be nurses and pianists. They were less dissembling. I was clever, I picked a virtue early and hung on to it. I was always doing things for another's good. The rest of my life I could push and pull at people with a clear conscience.*[6]

As a woman of noble character she frankly admits her human failings; still, she sticks to her moral ideals but ultimately ends up interfering in the life of other people. In her insistence on moral rectitude she does not spare even her husband who lived his life as she wished him to.

His mother's character has a profound influence on Gabe's mind, as he is more his mother's son than his father's. After reading the letter he determines that he "would do no violence to human life, not to another's, and not to my own"(3). His determination undoubtedly testifies to his altruistic intentions and purposes. At this early stage, he is little aware of the grim and harsh realities of life and has yet to begin his struggle for attainment of maturity and manhood. Moreover, he does not realize the distinction between the idealistic desire to do good to others and an actual engagement in others' affairs without jeopardizing one's own identity. Gabe is the pivotal character in the novel with whom all the other characters interact. His widower father is all too willing to shower his affection and money upon his son. He invites Gabe on Thanksgiving to New York as he is in need of his company to alleviate his feelings of loneliness and sadness. However, Gabe refuses the offer politely, but firmly, as he has some apprehension of an undesirable encroachment upon his personal freedom. Similarly, his relationship with the Herzes and Martha Reganhart, a young divorcee, turns out to be unsuccessful. In fact, the basic conflict faced by the protagonist in *Letting Go* is between the necessity and desire of involvement with others, and preservation of personal identity and freedom. The disparity in his lofty moral idealism and the normative values of the recognizable social world is a hindrance in his achievement of reconciliation and harmony.

Gabe meets Paul in Iowa city where both of them are graduate students in the university. He is at once attracted to this "harried young man rapidly losing contact with his own feelings" (3). Later on, his wife Libby Herz requests Gabe to help him when his car breaks down on the highway. Both of them share an interest in James's *The Portrait of a Lady* which Gabe had loaned to Paul. In this way, Gabe enters into the life of the Herzes. He comes to know that they are passing through a pathetic and sordid phase of their life. They are poverty-stricken and estranged from their families. His intention to help them is, no doubt, genuine initially but his altruism mysteriously takes the form of love towards Libby. In a weak moment, he holds Libby and kisses her, an act which proves to be a source of much embarrassment and chagrin for both of them. Interestingly, at this point of their relationship, James's *The Portrait of a Lady* is a focal point of their mutual interests and, thus, crystallizes the recurrent themes of moral consciousness and imperatives of conscience in the very beginning of the novel.

Gabe, like Neil, is much concerned about preservation of his moral integrity and selfhood, so much so that he withdraws suddenly whenever he finds his personal freedom threatened by any outside intrusion. Highly influenced by the literature of moral seriousness, he is morbidly conscious of the desirability of conscientious respect for individual privacy. But while attempting to do good to others he inadvertently intrudes upon others' life. He is so exasperated by the overlapping of these two motives in his mind that finally he begins the process of detaching himself from the interpersonal engagements. Nevertheless, his desire to do good and be good to others is beyond doubt. He tries his best to bring happiness in the life of the Herzes. He offers his car to Paul, arranges a job for him in the university, and, even after Libby's insulting outburst against him, he helps them whole-heartedly in their adoption of the child, Rachel. His concern for the welfare of Martha and her children is genuine. Finally, it is she who chooses to break off their relationship. He makes sincere efforts to keep his desolate father happy, although the old man makes heavy demands upon his son after the death of Mrs. Wallach. Gabe is perturbed by his persistent calls from New York asking him to visit him. Though he is not oblivious of his obligations to his father, he "was not prepared to surrender my [Gabe's] life to his [Dr. Wallach's]" (39).

Gabe's total involvement in benevolent and altruistic purposes is manifest in the sixth section of the novel appropriately titled "The Mad Crusader". After knowing that Theresa Haug is actually a married woman and is now unwilling to sign the documents necessary for the legal adoption of the child, he is in a feverish state of mind. Although he has made his final preparations to go to Europe, he decides to complete the process of adoption. With a firm resolve he deals with the rough and ignorant Mr. Bigoness, Theresa's husband. He implores him, persuades him, tempts him and even intimidates him to sign the documents but to no avail. Ultimately, when he realizes that he has almost failed in his purpose, he takes the little child, Rachel, to Bigoness's house and tries desperately to evoke human feelings in him. After a lot of confusion and altercation, he finally collapses on his knees and suffers a nervous breakdown. At this stage, he has reached his final moment of revelation of truth. Ironically, the bitter reality which he had been evading all his life dawns upon him now with full force and conviction. He realizes that it is almost impossible to do good without involvement with others and that complete detachment and separation from the vast sea of mankind is neither desirable nor feasible. After fulfilling his obligations, he leaves for Europe to recuperate from the shock of his encounter with the evil hidden under the surface of normalcy. Sanford Pinsker remarks: "Only Gabe is left to drift as uncommitted at the end of the novel as he was at the beginning."[7] But his contention does not seem to be true, as Gabe has learnt a lot from his experience and he is a wiser and mature person at the end of the novel.

Though Gabe shares a number of traits with the protagonists of *Goodbye, Columbus* and the earlier short stories, the choices for him are not as simple and clear as for Neil, Ozzie Freedman or Eli Peck. His personality is shrouded in mystery and ambiguity and of all the characters in the novel he is the most difficult to define and evaluate. Despite his willingness to gain the experience of felt life and to enhance the happiness of others, he is afraid of taking a direct plunge in the process of engagement with others. His romantic notions and idealistic approach in dealing with interpersonal relationships prevent him from confronting the social forces directly and squarely.

Rodgers compares Gabe to Gilbert Osmond of *The Portrait of a Lady* "in his manipulation of others and in his tendency to take advantage of their weaknesses", and to Isabel Archer in his reluctance to participate actively in the experience of life.[8] Though there does not seem any overt manipulation of others for some evil purpose on his part, Gabe is certainly confused and ambiguous in his response to his immediate society, which can be attributed to his strained sense of moral idealism and reluctance to loose his identity. His evaluation of human relationships is based on some distorted and superficial assumptions. He himself admits, "It was beginning to seem that toward those for whom I felt no strong sentiment, I gravitated; where sentiment existed, I ran" (30). He is fully aware that his response to his father's request for his company falls short of his expectations and that the lonely man deserves more in his old age. Greatly exasperated by his attitude, Dr.Wallach says about his son, "He was just like his mother – cold. He hated them both for leaving him" (486). But evidently the old man is sad and bitter because of the vacuum in his life caused by his wife's death, who was a source of the necessary dynamic in his life. Otherwise he is tender and affectionate to his son.

Then there is Gabe's brief and dismal love affair with Marjorie Howells, a "sweet empty-headed girl" (28). After a couple of nights of sexual pleasures he decides to end the affair and asks her to leave his apartment without apparently giving any consideration to the emotional disturbance his action would cause. She leaves his apartment in his absence and leaves a bitter note for him saying, "I gave too much to you. I don't think anybody can ever hurt me the way you have. I don't know what I'll do" (47). But in her sexual promiscuity (there is a hint of her sexual adventure with Paul also) she appears more akin to such later heroines of Roth as Mary Jane Reed of *Portnoy's Complaint*, Sharon Shatsky of *My Life as a Man* and Birgitta Svanstrom of *The Professor of Desire*. Gabe and Howells both are aware of the real nature of their affair from the very beginning. Gabe does not display any signs of committing himself to her and, obviously, the affair appears to be nothing more than a brief carnal encounter. He retorts in the course of their argumentation: "We used each other" (40).

It is true that Gabe appears to be self-centered and casual in his personal relationships. But this is attributable to his tendency to escape his entanglements with others at the slightest hint of danger to his selfhood and individuality. As Jones and Nance point out, Gabe is not able to maintain intimate relationships with others because "he equates intimacy with the surrender of the self, of separateness."[9] In the matters of human relationships, he seems to believe in the tenets of D.H. Lawrence who advocates a safe distance in interpersonal relationships to achieve perfect balance and harmony. The real and everlasting love relationship consists in, as Rupert Birkin says in *Women in Love*, "maintaining of the self in mystic balance and integrity – like a star balanced with another star."[10]

As far as Paul and Libby are concerned, Gabe feels genuine sympathy for them since their first meeting in Iowa. But later he impulsively kisses her little realizing that he is inadvertently igniting her wild romantic notions of freedom from her wretched life. Thus, he unnecessarily adds much pain and confusion in their already sordid life. He is much like Isabel, at least, in this respect; he fails to understand other's motives and is confused about his own. In fact, his lofty ideals of moral scruples partly inherited from his mother and partly derived from his literary background are an obstacle in his comprehension of existential reality. It cannot be denied that he is aware of his obligations and responsibilities to the other people. But he overlaps his priorities :

> Soon I was worrying all over again as to the whereabouts of Marge Howells. I should have pulled over to Herz to ask ... But what business of mine was she any more? If Marge Howells wanted to run, let her run! If my father wanted to pine, let him pine! If Libby Herz wanted to weep, let her weep! (58)

His irritation reveals, on the one hand, his inability to understand his relationships with these characters and, on the other, his deep concern and anxiety about them.

In these circumstances, Martha Reganhart seems a ray of hope to him. Her stolid, extrovert and energetic personality is in sharp contrast to sick and neurotic Libby. A young divorcee, she is grappling with hostile circumstances to bring up her two children, Cynthia and Markie. Gabe says of her: "... Martha Reganhart began to loom in my head – and subsequently in my heart too – as a green, watery spot in a dry land; I felt in her something solid to which I could anchor my wandering and strained affections" (169). While cohabiting with her, he seems to be relieved of his conflict between obligation to others and his personal freedom, as Martha at this stage assures him that she would not insist on marriage. To testify the solemnity of their relationship they invite the Herzes for dinner which turns out to be disastrous. After a lot of furor and misunderstanding Paul and Libby leave them.

The ensuing interchange between Gabe and Martha brings to light her bitterness against the world and she cries in the end exhorting Gabe to marry her: "Oh Gabe, the hell with Theresa Haug. The hell with all that Armagnac. I want you to marry me or give me up. I'm too old to screw around like this" (321). In the end, the decision to end the relationship is entirely hers. But Gabe's untempered idealism prevents him in realizing the delicate balance between separateness and engagement.

Several critics have pointed out Gabe's inaction and indecisiveness. But once he realizes the presence of lurking evil beneath the shining surface of society, he can act decisively. In the chapter "The Mad Crusader", he introspects :

> The same impulse that had led him to want to tidy up certain messy lives had led him also to turn his back upon others that threatened to engulf his own. He had finally come to recognize in himself a certain dread of the savageness of life. Tenderness, grace, affection: they struck him now as toys with which he had set about to hammer away at mountains. (529)

In his encounter with the contemporary social reality he discovers the existence of evil in all its manifest forms. His commitment to community and society being absolute, he realizes the necessity of some modification in his response to the adverse forces. He does not compromise with his moral ideals, rather, he remains firm and steadfast in his ethical stand. After comprehending the true nature of social reality, he acts with determination and resolve to ensure the adoption of the child, Rachel, for the Herzes. At the end of the novel, he has comprehended the nature of the conflict between ethical ideals of the individual and normative values of society. Moreover, he succeeds in affirming his value system dauntlessly.

Roth skillfully manipulates his narrative techniques to examine the ethical conflicts of his characters from different perspectives. The second section of the novel entitled "Paul Loves Libby" is narrated in third person and here his whole focus is on Paul and Libby. Paul is a sort of counterpart of Gabe who traverses an alternate trajectory, though both of them reach the same point in the process of attaining selfhood and identity. Paul and Libby have married against the wishes of their parents; consequently, they are totally estranged from them. Libby's parents never forgive their daughter for marrying a Jewish boy. When out of sheer financial necessity she writes a letter to her father for help, his reply is sarcastic and venomous :

> Surely to one with an inspiration so inhuman, I can only reiterate that neither aid nor good wishes can be expected, now or in the days to come, from this quarter. Obligations are reciprocal, and when one party has failed another, the cessation of obligatory feelings from the injured can be designated with no word other than Justice; certainly with none of the words you suggest. My obligations, Mrs. Herz, are to sons and daughters, family and Church, Christ and country, and not to Jewish housewives in Detroit. (141)

Evidently, Libby has nowhere to turn to for help and sympathy except Paul, who, unfortunately, is barely able to support her. It is but natural that in Gabe she sees a kind of savior who can deliver her from her wretched circumstances. Despite Paul's solicitude and concern, her wish for a contended and happy life remains unfulfilled. John N. McDaniel is of the opinion that Paul does not feel love for Libby; rather he feels the "same duty that he believes he owes his family."[11] In fact, Libby herself complains to her psychoanalyst that Paul does not love her. On some occasions he even encourages her to commit adultery with Gabe so that the latter can save her from her miserable life and provide her some happiness and joy. Though she always tries to keep her husband happy, she is a constant source of anxiety and tension for him.

Given her temperament and circumstances, Libby naturally discerns a ray of hope in Gabe and commits the mistake of succumbing to her weaker impulses. Gabe is mysteriously attracted to her. In her apartment he gives way to his instincts impulsively: "I sat down on the edge of the bed and without too much confusion, we kissed each other. We held together afterwards, but for only a second" (57). Later on, this simple kiss proves a source of much embarrassment and confusion for both of them. But her fidelity to Paul is as unshaken as ever.

In a way, the pathetic situation of Libby can be attributed more to her own temperament than her choice of marrying Paul. She is so confused that she is herself not sure of her yearnings. Initially, when she gets pregnant she is of the opinion that they cannot afford a child and gets an abortion. Afterwards when she needs a child, it is not medically advisable for her to get pregnant due to her bad kidneys. In her miserable state she desperately wants a child. Her aimlessness and mental vacuity are explicit in her utterance: "Oh I want a baby or something. I want a dog or a TV. Paulie, I can't do anything" (246). After they adopt the child, Rachel, there seems a ray of hope and happiness in their life.

Paul's circumstances are different from Gabe's. Once having decided to marry Libby, he remains firm in his commitment whatever be the consequences. His parents never recover from the shock of their son's marrying a Catholic girl. He, like Libby, is alienated from his parents and expects little help from his father. Over a long span of suffering and misery, he has developed a kind of stoic attitude and appears to have accepted unhappiness as an essential condition of life. In his rigidity and self-righteousness, he is more like Lucy Nelson of *When She was Good* than Gabe. He nourishes some misconceived opinions about himself and thinks that "he was of another order of men" (408). Even his uncles Asher and Jerry, despite their best efforts, fail to dissuade him from marrying Libby.

Asher, in his characteristically rude and obscene language, exhorts him to conform to the normative values of society:

> Things come and go, and you have got to be a receptacle, let them pass right through. Otherwise death will be a misery for you, boy; I'd hate to see it. What are you going to grow up to be, a canner of experience? You going to stick plugs in at either end of your life? Let it flow, let it go. Wait and accept and learn to pull the hand away. Don't clutch! (83).

What Asher does not realize is that in his own peculiar and funny way he is presenting the image of modern man caught in the whirlwind of absurd forces. He himself is a typical victim-figure in contemporary society for whom all values have lost their meaning and significance. He frankly admits; "I don't bottle experience. I'm interested in the flow. I'll take the shape the world gives me" (83). Ironically but definitely, he is evoking the image of "jelly-fish" as suggested by Tony Tanner in relation to the predicament of modern man.[12] In the bar they see a drunken youngster in the arms of a seventy-year old alcoholic saying, "Nothing in the world is irretrievable" (83). The words are highly suggestive and meaningful. Roth seems to suggest that the illusion of escape from social involvement is the root cause of much unhappiness and misery in this world. One is so lost in the maze of the confounding elements of experience that to start all over again is not feasible for an ordinary human being. The lonely traveler of Robert Frost knows better, when he is convinced that choices are irrevocable and a wrong decision makes "all the difference."[13]

But Asher is a different kind of man. Like Leo Patimkin in *Goodbye, Columbus,* he is a typical Jewish failure. However, Leo can still travel distances to sell bulbs and maintain his wife and child. Asher, on the other hand, lives a sterile and meaningless life. His degradation is complete and he is past any hope of regeneration. Roth purposely shows us a glimpse of his life of moral depravity and waste. In a way, he is a point of reference to highlight Paul's firm belief in his ethical tenets. Instead of being convinced by his exhortations not to marry Libby, Paul is disgusted with Asher's obscenity, indignity and moral turpitude. He is shocked that Asher cannot understand his simple human instinct of love for Libby. His uncle Jerry is more experienced and mature. He strikes the right note when he says, "We're not dealing with the mind, with the practical senses anyway. This is the mysterious, spontaneous choice – the choice of the heart. The unencumbered heart.... The heart, Paul, knows" (92). The words are highly suggestive and show that Roth's ethical tenets originate from the instinctive truth of the heart.

Paul's idealism is broader and deeper, and is determined by his heart-felt convictions rather than any metaphysical principles. In this connection, Rodgers pertinently points out that Paul Herz's last name means "heart" in Yiddish.[14] In *Letting Go* like *Goodbye, Columbus* and the short stories Roth puts his emphasis on instinctive and spontaneous moral attributes like compassion, sympathy and love which are a true measurement of moral consciousness and not on any artificial and logical principles. Despite Paul's harrowing circumstances, he is never oblivious of his duty and obligations to Libby and his parents. He pays a visit to his ailing father in Brooklyn. In the railway station in New York, he contemplates his predicament and gives vent to his feelings of failure and exhaustion :

> He had only to climb aboard and get off in Wilmington, Baltimore, or Miami Beach. Washington

> ... get a little room somewhere, get a job in some government office, and disappear. Start making a life not on the basis of what he dreamed he was, or thought he was supposed to be, or what literature, philosophy, friends, enemies, wife, parents told him he must be, but simply in terms of his own possibilities. (412-13)

Thus, the conflict in his soul is between letting go and hanging on, between the convictions of the heart and the demands of the surrounding society. Halio is of the opinion that in case of many of Roth's protagonists "moral conscience conflicts with hedonistic inclination."[15] But his observation appears to be more appropriate in the case of Roth's later protagonists like Portnoy and David Kepesh.

In *Letting Go,* the whole emphasis is on the problem of social involvement and its ethical ramifications. Here the conflict is between the need for the preservation of personal freedom and the necessity of social engagement. Paul chooses the arduous course of fulfilling his responsibilities and stifles his urge for freedom and escape. On the occasion of his father's funeral when he passionately embraces his mother, his emotions get the better of him and he realizes his actual place in the larger scheme of things. In this brief moment, as if in an epiphany, truth is revealed to him through intense imaginative experience. When his mother kisses him, all of his conflicts, frustrations and sorrows dissolve in that small instant and he achieves peace and harmony, though temporarily. His predicament is exactly similar to that of Tommy Wilhelm of Bellow's *Seize the Day*. A typical victim of circumstances, Tommy comprehends the working of existential forces through emotional experience at the end of the novel. Paul is able to comprehend, at last, the social and ethical compulsions of the individual in the midst of a wider cosmic design:

> While his mother kissed his neck and moaned his name, he saw his place in the world. Yes. And the world itself - without admiration, without pity. Yes! Oh Yes! What he saw filled him for a moment with strength.... For his truth was revealed to him, his final premise melted away. What he had taken for order was chaos. Justice was illusion. Abraham and Isaac were one. His eyes opened, and in the midst of those faces – the faces of his dream, the faces of the bums, all the faces that had forever encircled him – he felt no humiliation and no shame. Their eyes no longer overpowered him. He felt himself under a wider beam. (452)

He apprehends the mysterious forces of the world and the individual's situation amid these forces not through the rational mind but through heart. He gracefully accepts life as it is, and his own role and place in it. Apparently, he passes through his moral ordeal triumphantly and is better equipped to face existential reality at the end of the novel.

But as indicated earlier, Paul can be viewed as a point of reference in the novel to bring in sharp focus the complex personality of Gabe. Paul, seen in this perspective, might as well represent the alternative course of Gabe's choices. It can be safely assumed that Gabe has reached a higher level of ethical evolution since he chooses to act resolutely in order to bring about necessary modifications in his response. Obviously, Roth intended Gabe to be the center of major themes and concerns of the novel.

Roth firmly believes that man's quest for salvation essentially passes through his family and society. McDaniel convincingly argues that in *Letting Go* Roth is exploring "the genuine difficulties of active self-assertion within the community."[16] Besides the primary relationship of man and woman, Roth deals with the vital relationship of parents and children in his books. As far as parents-children relationship is concerned, the basic issues involved are mutual faith, respect for each other's individuality and reciprocal expectations and demands. In *Letting Go* Roth has tried to explore all these issues through different sets of parents and children. This conflict surfaces very early in the novel when Gabe's father, out of sheer loneliness, craves for his son's company. He passionately pleads his son to visit him in New York on Thanksgiving and on his refusal accuses him of running away intentionally from him. Though tender and affectionate to his father, Gabe considers his father's insistence as an unjustified demand on his part. He wants to preserve his personal freedom and is "not prepared to surrender" his life to his father (39).

Like most of the father-figures in Roth's fiction, Dr.Gabe is an assiduous, self-sacrificing and affectionate person though he fails to understand his son's feelings. His mother categorically admits in her last letter to Gabe: "*Whatever unhappiness has been in our family springs from me. Please don't blame it on your father however I may have encouraged you over the years.*" (2) In fact, Gabe's mother is on the extreme end of the moral spectrum inasmuch as she vehemently adheres to her higher ethical ideals. After her death Dr. Gabe feels loneliness and craves for his son's company. But fortunately for Gabe, his emotions divert to an alcoholic, Fay Silberman, whom he decides to marry. He has somehow reconciled to the fact that "all sons leave their fathers" (487). Outwardly, he enjoys with his friends and even undertakes a tour of Europe, yet he feels lonely and sad.

Through intimate filial relationships Roth explores the germination and the evolution of the value system of his protagonists. In his fiction the children more often than not display a lack of communication with their fathers in spite of their love and reverence for them. Portnoy, for all his regards for his father, not infrequently gives vent to his feelings of discontent and resentment against him. Similar is the case with Zuckerman, Lucy and Paul. This may be attributed to their apprehension of total control of their life by their fathers. Leonard Herz, though on his death bed, is never able to reconcile to the marriage of his son, Paul, with a Catholic girl. In a frantic effort to prevent his marriage with Libby he asks Asher and Jerry to dissuade him. But Paul is acutely conscious of his responsibility towards Libby with whom he has had premarital sexual relations, and so he remains committed to her. At the same time he is always aware of his duty and obligation towards his parents. Completely opposed to these Jewish fathers is Mr.DeWitt, Libby's Gentile father. His sarcastically vindictive attitude is clear from his letter to his daughter in response to her request for help. He has not forgiven her for marrying a Jewish boy. Naturally, Libby feels nothing but hatred and disgust for her parents.

The problem of parent-children relationship is analyzed in a different perspective in the case of Martha Reganhart. In the majority of Roth's novels, the filial relationships are evaluated by the offspring; but here they are examined from the point of view of the young mother. Martha is a young divorcee who is struggling alone in the world to bring up her children. She sacrifices her personal freedom for her children and has no intention of marrying any of her suitors. But when her former husband suddenly comes back to claim his children she allows Cynthia and Markie to live with him. Unfortunately, Markie dies tragically in a minor accident. Thus, through this episode Roth seems to hint at Martha's nemesis. He firmly believes that virtues like affection, self-sacrifice and generosity are indispensable for vital and lasting filial bonds.

In *Letting Go* Roth seems to suggest that family as the most vital source of strength for the individual is disintegrating in contemporary American society, and the individual is left with his own meager resources to face hostile forces. The most intense demonstration of this phenomenon is found in *When She Was Good,* where Lucy Nelson takes on the whole society single-handedly to prove her moral superiority. There are other instances of the severance of domestic ties in Roth's novels. In *Zuckerman Unbound* the protagonist, rejected by his brother and separated from his wife is haunted by the curse of his dying father. Far from celebrating this loss of interpersonal communion in the modern society on any ground, Roth laments the dissolution of familial bonds.

In Roth's fiction father-figures are, for the most part, portrayed in warm and congenial terms. Dr. Gabe, Jack Portnoy, Abe Kepesh and Roth's own father in *Patrimony* are all loving and sincere fathers. When there are no real fathers Roth presents father figures or the surrogate fathers who give guidance, encouragement and consolation to the protagonists. For example, Mr. Patimkin in *Goodbye Columbus,* Uncle Jerry in *Letting Go,* E.I. Lonoff in *The Ghost Writer,* and Tarnopol's brother Moe in *My Life as a Man* are elderly father figures giving assurance and solace to the protagonist at a critical juncture of his life. But at the same time, Roth is never oblivious of the fact that tensions and conflicts in interpersonal relationships are inevitable and unavoidable. Unlike some of the heroes in contemporary fiction, his characters try to resolve these conflicts in the ambience of family and society instead of escaping into the void of absurdism. Whenever a character is isolated from his familial and social moorings he is burdened by a sense of rootlessness and guilt. This is a measurement of his strong emotional ties with his family which is a source of moral and psychological strength.

In *Letting Go* Roth earnestly deals with the complex issues of human relationships and their moral and psychological implications. The protagonist's choices are mapped not in isolated human conditions, but in the course of his actual participation in the familial and social intercourse. The basic conflict in the novel is between the protagonist's inherent ideals and the moral demands of the community. His choices are determined by his moral convictions notwithstanding the pressure of the society to conform to its normative values. The protagonist makes tremendous efforts to preserve his selfhood and moral integrity trying simultaneously to reconcile with the adverse outer forces. He gains a deep knowledge of and insight into the true nature of the constituent elements of social reality. Despite the pressure of existential forces, he sticks to his ethical values and does not deviate from his humanitarian course. In his ethical evolution Gabe, however, appears to be at a higher level than Neil. Here the Rothian protagonist has realized the necessity of involvement in the social process to achieve peace and harmony.

REFERENCES

1. Jay L. Halio, *Philip Roth Revisited* (New York: Twayne, 1992) 21.
2. Mark Shechner, "Jewish Writers," *Harward Guide to Contemporary American Writing*, ed. Daniel Hoffman (Delhi: Oxford UP, 1981) 233.
3. Judith Paterson Jones and Guinevera A. Nance, *Philip Roth* (New York: Ungar, 1981) 51.
4. George J. Searles, *The Fiction of Philip Roth and John Updike* (Carbondale: Southern Illinois UP, 1985) 38-39.
5. Bernard F. Rodgers, Jr., *Philip Roth* (Boston: Twayne, 1978) 48-49.
6. Philip Roth, *Letting Go* (London: Corgi, 1972) 2. All subsequent citations will be to the text as given in this edition and the page numbers will be indicated in parentheses appearing immediately after the quotation.
7. Sanford Pinsker, *The Comedy That 'Hoits': An Essay on the Fiction of Philip Roth* (Columbia: U of Missouri P, 1975) 42.

8. Rodgers 57.
9. Jones and Nance 45.
10. D.H. Lawrence, *Women in Love* (Harmondsworth, Penguin, 1976) 170.
11. John N. McDaniel, *The Fiction of Philip Roth* (Haddonfield, NJ. Haddonfield, 1974) 118.
12. Tony Tanner, *City of Words: American Fiction 1950-1970* (New York: Harper, 1971) 18.
13. Robert Frost, "The Road Not Taken", *Robert Frost: Selected Poems,* ed. Ian Hamilton (Harmondsworth: Penguin, 1977) 77.
14. Rodgers 52.
15. Halio 49.
16. McDaniel 84.

4

The Disastrous Collisions : *When She Was Good*

The second full-length novel of Philip Roth is distinct from most of his books in two ways: this is a book without any Jewish character in it, and its protagonist is a woman. The novel is in the form of naturalistic tradition of Theodore Dreiser, Frank Norris and Sinclair Lewis, and Roth painstakingly maintains a controlled and detached tone throughout the narrative. Surprisingly, of all his novels *When She Was Good* received the least attention when it was published in 1967. But later, many critics considered it a kind of contemporary document depicting the American social reality, which in Roth's opinion is difficult to express because of its absurdity and compexity. Roth asserts time and again in his essays and interviews that the artist's purpose is to arouse the moral awareness of the reader through his depiction of the contemporary social reality. In *When She Was Good,* he presents the clash between the ethical values of the individual and those of his community.

The novel narrates the tale of an American Midwestern girl driven mad by single-minded adherence to her self-righteous notions of right and wrong. In his previous novel, *Letting Go,* Roth delineates the protagonist's dilemma of involvement in social interaction and the preservation of his personal freedom and identity. In *When She Was Good,* he explores the consequences of the lonely and bitter struggle of an individual who, convinced of her own moral superiority, fails to understand the true nature of existential reality. Initially, the novel was criticized by many critics as banal, dull, 'laboured' and 'lifeless'.[1] Hermione Lee calls it the "most uncharacteristic and uninspired of his books" in which the writer has tried, though unsuccessfully, to portray the Midwestern Gentile milieu.[2] But now that the critical opinion of Roth's fiction is well-established, it is considered to be one of the greatest novels by Philip Roth.

Though Roth's main concern in his fiction is ethical implications of the individual's experience in family and society, in no other novel does he explore the nature of moral values so intensively and comprehensively as in *When She Was Good*. At one level, Lucy appears to be the epitome of goodness whereas on the other, she seems to assume the role of a self-righteous, horrid monster. Caught in the value system of a Midwestern small town, she overlaps her own ethical convictions and beliefs, howsoever justified, and the pragmatic demands of the society. Like the protagonists of *Goodbye, Columbus* and *Letting Go,* Lucy faces the conflict between her idealistic values and compulsions of existential reality; but here she stretches her notions of moral rectitude too far. She not only tends to follow the strict self-improvised moral principles but also insists on others to comply with her. As a consequence of her failure to understand and imbibe existential reality, she is isolated and alienated from her society. The achievement of spiritual harmony and peace seems to be a remote possibility in her case, since in her egotistic fury she refuses to participate in the essential human process and negates the humanitarian virtues of forgiveness and kindness.

In *When She Was Good* as in all his fiction, Roth presents his ethical concerns through the interpersonal relationships in family and society. Except his autobiographical book, *Patrimony,* nowhere is Roth more concerned with the theme of parents-children relationship as in this novel. As Roth himself admits in *Reading Myself and Others, When She Was Good* and *Portnoy's Complaint* deal with the same theme of "warfare between parents and children."[3] He points out the striking similarities in *When She Was Good* and *Portnoy's Complaint*: "Wholly antithetic in cultural and moral orientation, she is, in her imprisoning passion and in the role she assumes of the enraged offspring, very much his soul mate."[4] The difference in *Portnoy's Complaint* and *When She Was Good* is superficial inasmuch as Portnoy is rallying against his Jewish milieu while Lucy's rage is against the value system of a small Midwestern Protestant society. Nevertheless, the nature of conflict is different in these books; in *Portnoy's Complaint* the conflict is mostly internal and psychological whereas in *When She Was Good* it is predominantly external, between Lucy and the whole system notwithstanding her miserable isolation in the later part of the novel. Under the suffocating burden of parental authority, Portnoy has recourse to sexual gratification whereas Lucy, convinced of her own goodness, launches a fierce attack on all those around her. But ultimately, both of them find themselves in the same predicament. Totally exhausted by his passions and conflicts, Portnoy collapses in the couch of his psychoanalyst, Dr. Spielvogel, and Lucy destroys herself in a schizophrenic frenzy.

While examining female characters in Roth's fiction, Mary Allen comes down heavily on Lucy, branding her as a kind of despicable monster:

> But the fact that Lucy is offered an abortion and refuses it begins to establish that she is more a

victimizer than an innocent victim. Her desire for revenge along with the bleakness of her surroundings, to which she does not bring the imagination that enlivens her husband, work together to make her one of the super bitches of the sixties."[5]

But this is stretching the point too far. Admittedly, Lucy has her shortcomings, but her reactions more often than not are a by-product of her family upbringing. Despite his best intentions Willard Carroll, her grandfather, is an ineffectual head of the family and Lucy's accusation in the last part of the novel that he is an "impotent and helpless man," though the outcry of an anguished soul, has some grain of truth in it.[6] For her father she has Whitey, a "no-good low-life weakling" who is a parasite on Willard and instead of supporting his family squanders his time and money drinking in Earl's Dugout (40). Her mother Myra tolerates his wayward behavior submissively and never grumbles or revolts against him. Lucy naively cherishes the idea of a perfect family in which men are expected to discharge their duties and responsibilities dauntlessly. Having grown up in the forties, she naively nurses the illusion of an ideal family where the men and women play their specified roles. Even Roth opines in *Reading Myself and Others* that her illusory notions are more or less typical in this respect and not peculiar or abnormal in American society in the fifties :

> For it has always seemed to me that though we are, to be sure, not a nation of Lucy Nelsons, there is a strong American inclination to respond to life like Lucy Nelson – an inclination to reduce the complexities and mysteries of living to the most simple-minded and childish issues of right and wrong.[7]

As if her father and grandfather were not enough for her, she chooses Roy as her husband who, ironically, turns out to be exactly the kind of man Lucy abhors vehemently. Roy is a lazy and immature person who seems to be unable to bear the burden of his wife and child and runs away to his uncle Julian for emotional support on every occasion. Thus, Lucy's hopes of an ideal man in her life are shattered: "And yet it was what she had prayed for all her life – that a man stern, serious, strong and prudent would be the husband of her mother, and the father to herself" (228). Interestingly, there is only one male character in the novel who fulfills her criteria of a man, and he is Julian Sowerby whom Lucy hates for his shrewdness and hypocrisy. Disgruntled with the attitude of the members of her family, she starts suspecting the small-town ethical values of her immediate society and her suspicions like "Ozzie's questions about normative values and beliefs, threaten the social order of her elders."[8] But whereas innocent Ozzie, though rebellious, is forgiven by his elders, Lucy as a grown-up woman is castigated, suppressed, and finally marginalized by the male dominated society.

Given her rebellious and rigid temperament, Lucy refuses to be a victim like her mother and unintentionally assumes the role of the victimizer: "But she hated suffering as much as she hated those who made her suffer, and she always would" (84). She even tries conversion to Catholicism and "dedicated herself to a life of submission, humility, silence and suffering" till the incident when her father in a drunken state throws away the pan of water in which her mother was soaking her feet (81). Her adoption of noble Christian virtues, however, is short-lived and temporary: "After calling upon Saint Teresa of Lisieux and Our Lord – and getting no reply – she called the police" (81). As if this shock was not enough for the family, on another occasion she bolts her father out of the house. When Whitey sees his pregnant daughter shutting him out he feels so abashed and humiliated that he leaves Willard's house for good only to return after her death. Thus, her sense of ethical superiority over others is explicitly shown by the author in the very beginning of the novel.

Like Neil, Gabe, and Paul, Lucy cherishes some idealistic notions of ethical conduct which should govern the life of the people around her. Sanford Pinsker compares her to the heroine of *Madame Bovary* in her illusory concept of reality.[9] The choices before her are limited: either to follow her ideals of ethical principles defying all the familial and social exhortations, or to conform to the small-town value system thrust upon her by the society and deny herself the possibility of self-fulfillment and harmony. Without much hesitation she chooses the former and refuses staunchly to be the victim of the dehumanizing system little realizing the inevitable consequences of ignoring the pragmatic reality of recognizable social world. Her naive question, "Oh, why can't people be good?" demonstrates the narrow moral groove in which she has chosen to confine herself in her quest for selfhood and identity (288). In her assertion of simplistic notions of moral rectitude, she fails to see and imbibe the essential truth Father Damrosch preaches to her: "The world is imperfect.... Because we are weak, we are corrupt. Because we are sinners. Evil is the nature of mankind"(291).

Roth makes extensive use of irony in the portrayal of Lucy's complex personality. In the beginning of the novel, Lucy is projected as the good girl of the traditional nursery rhyme but as the novel progresses Roth makes more and more use of irony till the last part when she assumes the role of the bad girl turned horrid. Through the deft maneuvering of his narrative perspectives, Roth unfolds her character in such a way that just before her death she appears an obsessive beast though even then she is not altogether bereft of the reader's sympathy, and, perhaps, his creator's. To bring her moral stance in sharp focus, Roth in the first section of the book juxtaposes her goodness, honesty and courage to the passivity of Willard, irresponsibility of Whitey, utter submissiveness of her mother, and immaturity and waywardness of her husband, Roy.

Though her hatred and aggressiveness is discernible in the novel as early as when she calls the police to arrest her drunken father, the full force of her diabolic self-righteousness and egotism is felt in the third section of the novel. After returning to Fort Kean from their visit to their parents, Lucy gives vent to her disgust for Roy, her husband:

> "You worm! Don't you have any guts at all? Can't you stand on your own two feet, ever? You sponge! You leech! You weak, hopeless, spineless, coward! You will never change – you don't even *want* to change! You don't even know what I *mean* by change! (264).

Obviously, her disgust and hatred are a measure of her neurosis and morbidity. Her hatred for Julian is boundless, as in her opinion he is the symbol of the cruel and indifferent social system which thwarts the desires of the individual for self-fulfillment and demands conformity. As if to repudiate the whole social system she exposes his moral turpitude most unashamedly in the presence of all the members of his family. Lastly, she utters her misanthropic outburst against all men:

> Goodbye, protectors and defenders, heroes and saviors. You are no longer needed, you are no longer wanted – alas, you have been revealed for what you are. Farewell, farewell, philanderers and frauds, cowards and weaklings, cheaters and liars. Fathers and husbands, farewell! (305).

In her diabolic hatred she seems to forget that in her insistence on goodness she herself has deviated from the universal human virtues like righteousness, magnanimity and forgiveness. Unable to overcome the adverse outer forces or to reconcile with them, she recoils in her own interior dark recesses and, eventually, destroys herself.

Some critics are of the opinion that Lucy is an embodiment of the typical American destructive female character, a "ball-breaker of a bitch" (279) as Julian calls her. But when evaluated against the social and moral background of the fifties, it is evident that her conflict has much to do with the normative value system of a small Midwestern town – Liberty Center. The name of the town is ironical as Roth himself states that it was not accidental that he "came up with Liberty Center as the name for the town in which Lucy Nelson rejects every emancipating option in favor of a choice that only further subjugates her to her grievance and her rage."[10] Lucy's firm belief in the familiar myth prevalent in the mid-century American society of the perfect family with clearly defined masculine and feminine roles distorts her vision of the social reality. Keeping in view the moral and social ambience of the fifties when the watchwords for the young generation were duty, responsibility, and manhood, it is not surprising for a girl like Lucy to insist obsessively on these premium virtues.

Willard's only aim in life is to lead a civilized life, away from the savagery and illiteracy of his father in Iron City. The name is again symbolic as he has settled in Liberty Center in the hope of a life of enlightenment and emancipation, where Lucy finds herself entrapped in ethical principles as hard as iron. His ethical choices are clear and unambiguous in the very opening sentence of the novel: "Not to be rich, not to be famous, not to be mighty, not even to be happy, but to be civilized – that was the dream of his life"(3). He takes upon himself the role of the guide and protector of the lives of those dependent on him. While performing his duty and responsibility towards them, he inadvertently tries to control their life. "Failing to understand basic human individuality", Judith Paterson Jones and Guinevera A. Nance point out, "as his sister had, he deprives those whom he attempts to protect of their essential identity."[11] Albeit, in his innocence he claims that it is not feasible for him to mould and regulate the lives of others: "I am not God in heaven! I did not make the world! I cannot predict the future!"(40). Lucy's refusal to accept the basic fact of human relationships leads to her negation of sanctity of human life and, finally, to her annihilation. Amidst all the confusion in the end it is only Willard who reaffirms faith in human dignity and civilization.

George J. Searles rightly remarks that *When She Was Good* is a "probing exploration of family tensions."[12] Lucy's relationship with her parents is certainly the pivotal point of the novel. Having grown up in a broken family where her wayward father tortures her tender, timid, and subservient mother, she is mortified by isolation, marginalization and emotional insecurity. In her anger and resentment she gets her father arrested by the police and on another occasion she bolts him out of the house.

Actually, the idea of guilt which is the central theme in *Portnoy's Complaint* germinates in *When She Was Good*. Whitey is a victim of the Great Depression and has never been able to make it in America. Like Leo Patimkin in *Goodbye, Columbus* and Asher in *Letting Go*, he is a typical failure in the highly materialistic American society. Finally, unable to tolerate his condition he takes to drinking. His repeated resolutions to reform his life never prove successful as the sense of guilt again pushes him into the vicious circle of alcoholism. Willard concludes: "There is nothing the man can do. He is afflicted with himself. Like Ginny"(32). Ironically, in the house of his father-in-law whose sole commitment in life is to civilized behavior, Whitey inflicts violence against his own daughter. What saves him from utter damnation is his sense of repentance and regret, and a desire for reformation. His wish to reform his life, however, is thwarted by his dipsomania which finally lands him in the Florida State Prison on the charge of theft. But still, he nurses tender feelings towards his wife and daughter, as is evident in his last letter to Myra from the prison. Whitey does not even remotely resemble the typical father – figure in Roth's fiction, who is generally a self-sacrificing and responsible person.

The other most important male character in Lucy's life is Roy Bassart, her husband, who has spent sixteen months in The Aleutian Islands in the army. At the tender age of eighteen when she is lonely and isolated, she is seduced by him in Passion Paradise in most banal and unromantic circumstances and, consequently, gets pregnant. She insists on marrying Roy despite her parents' advice to have an abortion and apparently her own dislike of him even at this early stage. This only proves her rigidity and obstinacy. It is ironical, and even tragic, that Lucy chooses for her husband the kind of male she dislikes most – immature, irresponsible and weak. Roy is a day-dreaming drifter who is unable to support his family financially and emotionally, as is proved by his frequent visits to his uncle Julian whenever he confronts the slightest domestic problem. On one occasion he even suggests a kind of "temporary separation" from Lucy (211). Surprisingly enough, even before her marriage Lucy is certain that Roy is not a suitable person as a husband: "*She didn't want to marry him! He was the last person in the world she would ever want to marry*!"(169). In making her choice of marrying a person of Roy's character, she irrevocably plunges herself in a miserable condition. Irritated by his naive optimism and escapism, she wonders: "Who, after all, was Roy Bassart that he should feel no pain? Who was Roy Bassart that he should live a privileged existence? Who was Roy Bassart to be without responsibilities? This was not heaven. This was the world!" (271). Ironically, it is she who fails to grasp the pragmatic implications of her ethical choices.

In the last section of the novel when Lucy is engaged in an all out war with the social forces, Roy fails miserably to come to her rescue. Taking their child Edward with him he runs away to Uncle Julian and leaves her alone to fend for herself and her unborn child (she is pregnant for the second time). On this occasion, Roth's sympathy, though implicit, is with Lucy, as nowhere in his fiction does he approve of uncivilized and irresponsible behavior of a character in howsoever trying circumstances he may find himself. On such occasions, he expresses his disapproval of the character's diversion from humanistic virtues through gentle humor, irony or satire. However, as he himself asserts in *Reading Myself and Others,* he refrains from proposing explicitly any normative value system: "Now I won't claim that I am the one proposing those virtues here, since Daddy Will - as his family calls him - does not speak or stand for me in the novel any more than his grand daughter Lucy does."[13] Notwithstanding his consistently sustained narrative distance from the protagonist, Roth undoubtedly presupposes the reader's sympathy with Lucy when she, in the very presence of her husband, is waging a lonely battle against Julian who stands for the normative values of society:

> She kicked backward – the hand grasped and caught her ankle. Meanwhile Roy's face was moving up – to block her way! Her husband, who should be protecting her! defending her! shielding her! guarding her! instead stood between herself and her child, herself and her home, between herself and the life of a woman! (285).

Though confounded and miserable himself, Roy chooses to become a part of the ruthless and inhuman system and leaves her in the lurch. Driven into a corner,

Lucy loses all hopes of help from outside and fights alone against the physical force of Julian and her husband. In her schizophrenic violence against her husband, she reminds us of the heroine of Anita Desai's *Cry, the Peacock,* who pushes her husband down from the roof of the house. Significantly, the plot has come full circle, from Willard's commitment to civilization in the opening sentence of the novel to violence against and by a pregnant woman. Roy's choice is difficult to justify from any moral point of view.

The conflict in *When She Was Good,* like that in *Death of a Salesman* and *Invisible Man,* is between the lonely individual and the post-war American society which demands conformity to its hollow and false values. The protagonists of Arthur Miller and Ralph Ellison fight their lonely battle against the hostile social forces almost certain of their defeat. In the case of Lucy, these forces comprise largely the familial authority which is the microcosm of the recognizable social world. As has been mentioned earlier, the process of confrontation of self and the destructive elements of outer reality may lead to different kinds of consequences. The individual is either reduced to a formless "jelly-fish", utterly vulnerable and without identity, in the manner of the protagonists of Kafka; or after being victimized he tries to minimize the damage caused by the destructive experience, like the hero of Bellow's *Seize the Day*; or he is crushed psychologically, socially and even physically.[14] Lucy falls into the last category. Her condition is aggravated by her rigidity and egotism which lead her to the dark void of schizophrenia and ultimate self-destruction. John N. McDaniel rightly observes: "Lucy has been victimized by the banal normalcy of the Protestant Midwest ethic, and she has simply nothing with which to combat the banality of her existence, other than a misguided and ineffectual outrage."[15] But his contention that Lucy "acts out the drama of the absurd" is hard to accept.[16] Lucy does not move in a fantastic and grotesque void as, for example, Benny Profane in Thomas Pynchon's *V* or David Kepesh in *The Breast* do. Lucy firmly believes in her value system, but her rigidity, egotism and self-righteousness distort her vision of social and ethical values.

Lucy chooses not to be a victim like her mother, Myra, who tolerates patiently the injustice and even physical violence at the hands of her husband and still protects him on all occasions. Moreover, she expects Lucy to follow her suit. But Lucy firmly determines that "she would not repeat her mother's life, nor would her offspring repeat her own"(200). Commenting on his conception of the character of his protagonist, Roth says: "As I remember it, what most intrigued me at the outset was the utter victimization of this girl, whose misfortune it was to have been born into a world to which she believed herself morally superior."[17] Having made her choice not to follow her mother and be a victim, she embarks upon a mad crusade against what she believes injustice and evil around her. Ultimately, convinced of her own moral superiority she is outraged at others because of their reluctance to conform to the ethical code of conduct devised by herself: "I am their superior in every single way! People can call me all the names they want – I don't care! I have nothing to confess, because I am right and they are wrong and I will not be destroyed!"(84). Under the influence of some illusory notions of social morality, she refuses to see beyond the narrow confines of her ethical vision. She not only refuses adamantly to conform to the normative values of society but also inadvertently insists others to conform to her value system little realizing its narrow and limited range.

On the surface level, she resembles Gabe's mother who strives all her life to be "*Very Decent to People*" and is obsessed with the idea of goodness.[18] Seated on her high moral pedestal she reflects: "There were principles to be honored, values to respect, that went beyond blood relationships; but apparently they had no more knowledge of what it meant to be human than did her own family" (269-270). In the last part of the novel she finds herself in the typical predicament of modern man – lonely and isolated from her family and the community. She is alienated from her parents, grandparents, her husband and – if Roy's accusation is to be believed – from her own child, Edward, who is unwilling to live with her. Just like the typical postmodern "rebel-victim"[19] hero, she is imprisoned in her own egotistic cell: "Why would he come to her aid, when even those closest to her had turned against her? No, there was only one person she would rely upon; it was now as it had always been – the one to save her was herself"(304). Realizing the irreconcilable nature of the constituent elements of her conflict, she attacks all those around her. In her hallucination she first curses her father, then her husband and lastly all men who are, in her opinion, the perpetrators of evil. At this moment she has confined herself in self-devised ethical boundaries away from all the benevolent influences of humanity. Even her last words display her self-righteous and simplistic notions of right and wrong: "For they are wrong, and you are right, and there is no choice: the good must triumph in the end!"(307).

In *When She Was Good* Roth analyses the problem of ethical dilemma in all its dimensions. Significantly, he does not attempt to categorize his characters in watertight compartments of good and evil and prefers to suggest all the possible alternatives. Lucy is undoubtedly projected as a tragic figure having serious shortcomings in her character which ultimately cause her damnation. Apparently, her simplistic notions of ethical conduct in the social milieu of limited moral freedom prevent her from grasping and accepting the complexity of social reality and human nature. Particularly in her interpersonal demeanor she develops a kind of rigidity and obstinacy which proves to be her nemesis. Not only does she staunchly and obstinately adhere to her idea of truth, duty and goodness but also expects others to tread her path of virtue:

> Because they simply will not reform! They simply will not change! All they will do is get worse and worse! Why were they against a mother and a child? Why were they against a family, and a home, and love? Why were they against a beautiful life, and for an ugly one? Why did they fight her and mistreat her and deny her, when all she wanted was what was right! (302).

Firmly convinced of her own moral superiority to those who are better equipped than she is with worldly wisdom and experience, she gradually but definitely retreats into her own inner self from where she is unable to evaluate social reality clearly and objectively. Commenting on the predicament of Portnoy and Lucy, Roth says: "Those two characters, at the same time that they yearn for a more sociable and settled existence, are hell-bent on maintaining their isolation with all the rage and wildness in their arsenals."[20] When her father comes to know about her premarital pregnancy he does not so much as rebuke her (it was in 1950s, the years when freedom in sexual matters was considered unacceptable and unjustifiable in society). He mildly suggests an abortion as the best solution. But in her rigidity she does not agree to his proposal notwithstanding her dislike for Roy and decides to marry him. Even when in Fort Kean she discovers the fact of her pregnancy, she was sure that Roy was not for her. After their marriage she poignantly feels that Roy does not fit in her idea of a man and tries to improve him by stern discipline and admonitions. Ironically, the outer authority she vehemently despises in her own case is thrust upon Roy by her to make him a responsible man, father and husband. She appears to have forgotten the universal virtues of accepting and forgiving the common human weaknesses and failings.

As far as Roy is concerned, until now he loves her genuinely and has high opinion of her character: "She had courage. She had strength. She knew right from wrong. There was no one in the world like her. He felt privileged and honored to be her husband..." (213). How her egotism and pride leads her to misery is best illustrated by her utterance:

> He had settled at last into the daily business, whether he liked it or not, of being a father and a husband and a man ... and it was she alone who had made all this come about. This battle, too, she had fought and this battle, too, she had won, and yet it seemed that she had never in her life been miserable in the way that she was miserable now. (228)

In her moral rage she fails to realize that the actual cause of her misery is her negation of basic human virtues. In the last chapter, ironically entitled "Innocent", she castigates all the people closely related to her – Julian, Irene, Ellie and Roy. Her diabolic obsession with truth and justice is clearly reflected in her ferocious outburst against all of them. She venomously discloses the truth of Julian's adultery in front of his wife and young daughter. Roth seems to suggest here that the truth which poisons the life of so many people is not of much worth by any standard of morality. Naturally enough, she dies in freezing snow, which is symbolic of her cold soul devoid of any human warmth, kindness and sympathy.

As already indicated, Roth's characters invariably grow and set out on their quest for identity and selfhood in the matrix of family and society instead of escaping in the void of absurdism like the characters of many contemporary American novelists. In this regard, he says: "Not that I think that madness or alienation are glamorous or enviable conditions; being insane and feeling estranged don't accord with my conception of the good life."[21] In *When She Was Good* Roth intensively probes the intricate ramifications of human relationships and their ethical implications. The interactions of the minor characters with the central figure and with each other also form a part of the process of the evolution of his ethical vision. His concern with ethical values in this novel is evident in his observation that virtues of generosity, kindness and responsibility are "proposed as a way of life in the opening pages of the novel and continue to haunt the book thereafter (or so I intended)."[22]

The very opening sentence of the novel strikes the keynote of Roth's ethical preoccupations when Willard pronounces his choice of leading a civilized and decent life. This reminds us of Gabe's mother in *Letting Go,* who discloses to her son her intentions to do good to others. Willard has left the savage and ignorant world of his father in Iron City and settles down in Liberty Center in his pursuit of a noble and virtuous life. He is always haunted by his little mentally retarded sister who, ignored by his illiterate father, "lived and died beyond the reaches of human society"(12). But despite his best intentions, Willard is confronted by chaos and disorder in his family. He tolerates patiently the wayward and irresponsible behavior of his drunkard, "scheming, lying, thieving" son-in-law for sixteen long years, always pleading with Berta that the man would reform himself (40). In a grotesque incident Whitey pawns Willard's medals with Rankin's Pawnshop to get drunk in Earl's Dugout, but Willard still forgives him. Even after Lucy's death he is seen to be waiting for his middle-aged son-in-law to take him to his house so that he can start a new life. Alone in the graveyard he wonders, "Why be getting pneumonia and worrying myself sick – when all I did was good!"(39).

In fact, Willard hovers over the whole narrative of the novel in the manner of a vast mirror in which moral purpose and intentions of all other characters are reflected and magnified. Though Roth maintains a detached and objective tone throughout the novel, occasionally Willard appears to share the moral convictions of the writer. He never deviates from his virtuous path. However, in his innocence Willard fails to realize the fact that in doing good to others he is unconsciously striving to control their lives. The point Roth is trying to make in *When She Was Good,* according to Searles, is that "too much family, too much 'love', is as destructive as too little."[23] While pursuing his ideals of freedom and responsibility he inadvertently thrusts the tyranny of his love and authority upon all whom he tries to protect. In this connection, Roth writes, "The issue of authority over one's life is very much at the center of this novel, as it has been in my other fiction."[24] In this sense, Willard is the precursor of Sophie Portnoy who, through the ostensible promise of protection, tries to control indirectly her son's life. Portnoy lacks the will to protest; instead, he invents other channels to assert his freedom. Lucy, on the other hand, has the will and strength to oppose the dominance of Willard and refuses to accept the familiar myth of men as protectors and saviors. But when her rebellion crosses the socially defined moral boundaries, it brings about her doom.

The three female characters in the novel – Myra, Berta and Eleanor – may be viewed as three different points of reference for the purpose of focusing on the predicament of Lucy. Myra, in sharp contrast to Lucy, suffers all the injustice, cruelty and violence perpetrated by her husband; still, she tolerates her misfortune stoically. Her faith in his love is firm and unshakable. On the other hand, Berta is a down-to-earth, prudent and pragmatic woman who believes in social conformity. She always disapproves of the kind attitude of Willard and Myra towards Whitey and demands stern action against him to maintain her domestic decorum. Ellie reminds us of Brenda, a shallow and romantic girl who lives complacently in the material comforts provided by her father's millions. In Lucy's opinion she is "a vain and idiotic child" always thinking only of her hair, clothes and shoes (283). In the last crucial scene, instead of showing any sympathy for her old friend Lucy she calls her "crazy" and "insane" (282). Roth deliberately presents all these characters in the last section when Lucy attempts madly to retrieve her son from Julian's house. Through Lucy's self-righteous assertion of her goodness and complacency of others, Roth is able to explore ethical issues from different perspectives sustaining, at the same time, his solemn, detached and objective tone throughout the narrative.

Among all the minor characters, Julian Sowerby is the one whose moral stance seems hard to justify on any ground. More than any other character in the novel, he seems to be a part of the cruel and dehumanizing system which victimizes the individual and pushes him to the lowest level of human dignity. Ellie herself confides to Lucy that her father pays money to women for sleeping with him. Lucy smells evil in Julian very early when, on one occasion, she realizes with discomfiture that Julian was staring at her legs with more than usual interest. Naturally, she is aghast at the revelation of his adultery and exclaims, "What a disgusting cheat of a person!"(136). As she rightly suspects, Roy reposes more faith in Julian than his father as far as his domestic and personal matters are concerned. On one occasion he himself confesses that the suggestion of "temporary separation" from Lucy was offered to him by Julian (211). It is but natural that he becomes the main villain in her eyes. She is infuriated to learn of the threat of divorce from Julian's lawyer from Winnisaw. In the last chapter his conduct crosses all limits of decency when he literally assaults her, a pregnant woman half his age. Though it would be unwise to judge Julian through the distorted vision of Lucy, the fact remains that Roth does not approve of such hypocritical and adulterous characters. In this respect, he does not spare even Epstein, the protagonist of the story of the same title, who is a helpless victim of circumstances. Julian's wife and daughter know his true character but he is accepted because of his monetary power which he can use unscrupulously. He is the fittest person to thrive in the materialistic American society. The fact that he fails to express any emotion of guilt or repentance when his moral depravity is exposed before his wife and young daughter clearly indicates that he has gone beyond all hopes of redemption.

Though Julian is a sort of surrogate father of Roy inasmuch as he guides him in all his personal matters, yet he singularly lacks the humanitarian qualities generally found in the typical father figures in Roth's fiction. Lloyd Bassart, on the other hand, resembles the typical Rothian father figures such as Jack Portnoy, Abe Kepesh, Dr. Gabe and E.I. Lonoff in the sense that he is educated, scrupulous and civilized. Though he does not appear much in the novel, his moral stance is clear and unambiguous. When Roy confesses to him the truth of Lucy's pregnancy and asks him to expedite their marriage, he reflects, "Between a man doing the right thing and a man doing the wrong thing, there was really no choice..." (189).

In most of his novels Roth employs first person participatory point of view. The advantage of this technique is that "it permits total access to the inner workings of the central character's mind", and best suits him to delineate the conflicts of his highly sophisticated, urbane and intellectual protagonists. [25] On the other hand, in most of his short stories and realistic novels such as *When She Was Good, Zuckermann Unbound, The Anatomy*

Lesson, and *Sabbath's Theater*, he uses third person omniscient point of view. The reasons for this technique in *When She Was Good* are not far to seek. Here Roth intends to explore the moral and ethical implications of his protagonist's experience of social reality in a Midwestern Protestant town in America in the fifties. To analyze the predicament of Lucy from all perspectives, he relies heavily on irony. Consequently, his attitude varies from deep sympathy to utter disapproval of his victimized and obsessive heroine. In the first section of the novel, which is a kind of epilogue to the whole story of Lucy Nelson, he uses third person omniscient point of view though it shifts gradually from the author to Willard, and the whole plot is unfolded in a sort of pre-view as Willard sees it. Roth continues the same third person point of view in the second and third section of the novel in the naturalistic mode maintaining a detached and objective tone to allow the reader to judge for himself the propriety of Lucy's response to her social milieu. The last chapter which is a kind of epilogue is entitled "Innocent". The word is highly suggestive as at this stage Lucy, totally alienated from all human communication, wages her lonely battle in a state of schizophrenia just before her tragic end.

The language and syntax used by Roth in *When She Was Good* aptly convey the solemnity and seriousness of his thematic concerns. Some critics have pointed out that there is something artificial in his narrative and that "the uncomfortable syntax, the embarrassing archaisms" and "the dull choice of words" do not suit Roth's characteristic linguistic skill.[26] But we should not overlook the fact that in *When She Was Good* Roth is painstakingly trying to capture the linguistic overtones of the fifties to render his characters realistically. For this purpose, he skillfully manipulates his language to portray them in their different social and cultural context. Thus, the novel demonstrates his mastery of English language.

In *When She Was Good* Roth analyzes the moral predicament of the individual through delineating his encounter with the adverse social forces. Like her predecessors Neil and Gabe, Lucy cherishes some idealistic notions of social reality which are shattered at her very first encounter with the recognizable social world. In his encounter with the outer forces, Neil discovers the hollowness of contemporary social scene and gains a valuable insight into the true nature of these forces and his own response to them. Gabe strives to achieve his ethical ideals through interpersonal relationships only to discover in the end that involvement with others negates his own personal freedom and identity. In the portrayal of the character of Lucy, though, Roth seems to hint at the perils of egotism and self-righteousness in the assertion of one's ethical values. She chooses to oppose the inhuman system with all the resources at her disposal and to fight to a finish. Unable to overcome these destructive forces and refusing to bring about any kind of reconciliation with them, she turns her strength inward and destroys herself. The phase of suffering through which Lucy passes is an essential step in ethical evolution of the Rothian protagonist, since her fate demonstrates the necessity of the individual's reconciliation with ethical norms of the society for his self-fulfillment and spiritual harmony. Roth seems to suggest here that moral rectitude when pursued beyond a certain point itself proves a grave threat to individual as well as the social milieu which nourishes him. Lucy's ethical choices inevitably push her beyond her psychological and social boundaries and leads to her annihilation.

REFERENCES

1. Tony Tanner, *City of Words: American Fiction 1950-1970* (New York: Harper, 1971) 312.
2. Hermione Lee, *Philip Roth* (London: Methuen, 1982) 63.
3. Philip Roth, *Reading Myself and Others* (New York: Farrar, 1975) 26.
4. Roth, *Reading Myself* 26.

5. Mary Allen, "When She Was Good She Was Horrid", *The Necessary Blankness: Women in Major American Fiction of the Sixties* (Urbana: U of Illinois P, 1976). Rpt. in *Philip Roth*, ed. Harold Bloom (New York: Chelsea, 1986) 141.
6. Roth, *When She Was Good* (New York: Bantam, 1970) 294. All subsequent citations will be to the text as given in this edition and the page numbers will be indicated in parentheses appearing immediately after the quotation.
7. Quoted in Bernard F. Rodgers, Jr., *Philip Roth* (Boston: Twayne, 1978) 69.
8. Murray Baumgarten and Barbara Gottfried, *Understanding Philip Roth* (South Carolina: U of South Carolina P, 1990) 72.
9. Allen 141.
10. Roth, *Reading Myself* 28.
11. Judith Paterson Jones and Guinevera A. Nance, *Philip Roth* (New York: Ungar, 1981) 57.
12. George J. Searles, *The Fiction of Philip Roth and John Updike* (Carbondale: Southern Illinois UP, 1985) 39.
13. Roth, *Reading Myself* 27.
14. Tanner 18.
15. John N. McDaniel, *The Fiction of Philip Roth* (Haddonfield, NJ: Haddonfield, 1974) 128.
16. McDaniel 128.
17. Quoted in Granville Hicks, "A Bad Little Good Girl", rev. of *When She Was Good*, by Philip Roth, Saturday Review 17 June 1967: 25.
18. Roth, *Letting Go* (London: Corgi, 1972) 2.
19. Ihab Hassan, *Radical Innocence: Studies in the Contemporary American Novel* (Princeton: Princeton UP, 1961) 31.
20. Roth, *Reading Myself* 66.
21. Roth, *Reading Myself* 72.
22. Roth, *Reading Myself* 26.
23. Searles 41.
24. Roth, *Reading Myself* 28.
25. Searles 109.
26. Lee 63.

5

Fighting the Inner Demons : *Portioy's Complaint*

Portnoy's Complaint, published in 1969, is by far the most popular and widely read book written by Philip Roth and gained him much money, fame and even notoriety. The novel evoked a sharp reaction among the general public, and more particularly, the Jewish community. Philip Roth was charged with anti-Semitism and obscenity. The critics who had frowned upon what they considered as Jewish self-hatred in his earlier short stories and novels claimed to be justified in their scathing attack on this highly successful and controversial novel. Irving Howe found Roth's "creative vision deeply marred by vulgarity" as far as *Portnoy's Complaint* was concerned.[1] Roth himself does not pretend to be unaffected by this furor and controversy on his work, as is evident in his raking up the issue in his critical essays and even covertly in fictional form in his novel *Zuckerman Unbound* where the young writer is shown to have offended his Jewish family and community by writing a controversial book *Carnovsky*. Not surprisingly, in the course of so much emphasis on the ethnic dimensions of the novel, its artistic worth was grossly underrated. But now that the critical dust has settled, the general opinion about the merit of the book is well established.

Roth's main focus in *Portnoy's Complaint*, despite its Jewish milieu, is on the moral predicament of modern man confounded by the antagonistic forces in the microcosm of American society. Here, the problem of survival becomes more complex owing to the protagonist's inherited Jewish value system. Bernard F. Rodgers, Jr. emphatically contends that *Portnoy's Complaint* is "very much in the American grain in spite of its Jewish specifics" and that in its "essential conflicts, its themes, its characters, its language and comic technique" the novel belongs to the native American tradition.[2] It will not be inappropriate to assert that the basic issues in *Portnoy's Complaint* are too universal to be confined to any ethnic boundaries.

While discussing the genesis of the novel, Roth discloses in *Reading Myself and Others* that the novel "took shape out of the wreckage of four abandoned projects" on which he worked intensively in the 1960s: "The Jewboy", "The Nice Jewish Boy", "Portrait of the Artist" and "A Jewish Patient Begins His Analysis". [3] On close scrutiny of these early drafts, four motifs seem to emerge which form four corresponding dimensions of the moral predicament of the protagonist in the novel. The first is Portnoy's obsession with sexual pleasures, the second is his comprehension of social reality, the third is his problematic ethnicity, and the last dimension of his condition is his symptomatic response to his ethical dilemma. In *Portnoy' Complaint*, Roth is striving to bring into sharp focus the essential condition of modern man who, confronted with the onslaught of existential reality, manifests his malaise in such varied forms as physical violence, withdrawal into his own self, paranoia and self-destruction. In this novel, it is expressed predominantly in sexual gratification and narcissism. It is another matter that in this instance the individual happens to be a Jew in the American society.

Roth's fiction deals with the universal problem of man's moral dilemma in his society which demands conformity and normalcy and remains insensitive to the individual's demands. In Portnoy's case, however, his Jewishness itself is one of the main causes of his discomfiture and anguish. John N. McDaniel is also of the opinion that "Jewishness itself is partially to blame for Portnoy's crippledness...."[4] Throughout his long uninterrupted 'complaint' Portnoy seems to be haunted by a gnawing sense of guilt and repression at the hands of his parents who doggedly persuade him to cultivate those ethical values which are supposedly the exclusive attributes of 'The Chosen People'.

Nevertheless, on close scrutiny the novel is found to reveal issues and concerns far more serious and universal than what apparently meets the eye. Roth's fiction is thoroughly consistent thematically despite his experimentation with form and technique in some of his books like *Our Gang, The Great American Novel* and *Patrimony*. In *Portnoy's Complaint* also through his narrative technique of psychological case history, he analyzes the contemporary social reality in the tradition of such assimilated Jewish writers in America as Bellow, Mailer and Malamud. In Roth's fiction Jewishness serves as a frame of reference to evaluate and reinforce his experience of social reality. George J. Searles rightly observes that "Roth uses ethnicity as a framework or context within which to portray contemporary reality...."[5] The basic conflict in *Portnoy's Complaint*, like that in his earlier short stories and novels, is between the individual's yearning for personal freedom and spiritual harmony and his ethical compulsions in the surrounding society. What distinguishes it from his earlier novels is that here the protagonist is too confounded by his psychological anguish to realize the true nature of his moral dilemma till the point when the gravity of his condition necessitates for him the support of a psychoanalyst. Secondly, Roth has chosen a strikingly new form to express the dilemma and anguish of his protagonist – the confessional monologue of a patient on the couch of his psychoanalyst.

If interpreted in psychological terms, as critics like Bruno Bettelheim have tried to do, *Portnoy's Complaint* is comparatively easy to analyse.[6] Portnoy is a typical case of Oedipal complex, having excessive attachment with his mother – "The Most Unforgettable Character I've Met" – so much so that he attributes his sexual failure with Naomi to her resemblance with his mother.[7] The taboos and repressions let loose upon him by his mother to make him "a nice Jewish boy" cause a severe sense of guilt in him which leads him to excessive indulgence in masturbation in adolescence and heterosexual pleasures in youth (120). Due to the ethnic impressions of his past familial life he compulsively chooses *shikses* for his sexual gratification. Instead of providing any respite to his tortured mind, his carnal orgies again intensify his self-loathing and guilt plunging him in severe mortification and agony. In this way, he is entrapped in a vicious circle and unable to tolerate his torments any more seeks the help of his psychoanalyst.

But the evaluation of Portnoy's predicament in purely psychological terms is grossly inadequate as well as misleading. As a matter of fact, the moral and social issues form the thematic core of the novel, which also link it to Roth's previous novels. As Roth himself explains in *Reading Myself and Others*, the earlier draft of the novel entitled "The Jewboy" was mainly concerned with sexual fantasy of the hero, the second draft titled "The Nice Jewish Boy" dealt with moral dimension of his problems, and the other draft titled "Portrait of the Artist" depicted the social reality of the hero.[8] In *Portnoy's Complaint* he successfully synthesizes all these elements to bring into sharp focus the predicament of his protagonist in its totality and complexity. Portnoy's Oedipal attachment with his mother, his obsession with his Jewishness and his dissolute life combine to exclude the possibility of any meaningful reconciliation with his surrounding society.

The genesis of Portnoy's problems can be traced back to his early childhood when his parents, especially his mother, exert their authority to inculcate in him the good traits of character traditionally associated with the Jewish culture, in other words, to make him a "nice Jewish boy"(120). Sophie Portnoy, like Gabe's mother in *Letting Go,* is obsessed with the idea of goodness. She "herself had to admit that it might even be that she was actually too good"(11). In the manner of Willard Carroll in *When She Was Good,* she inadvertently interferes in the lives of all those around her and never misses the slightest opportunity to castigate whosoever deviates from the sacred Jewish code of conduct, especially Portnoy, who is the central figure of her affections and expectations. For instance, he is haunted by the sight of his mother brandishing a knife over him for not eating his food. He laments, "When I am bad I am locked out of the apartment. I stand at the door hammering and hammering until I swear I will turn over a new leaf. But what is it I have done?"(13). Though he resents his parents' exhortations to be good, it is paradoxically true that he himself is obsessed with the desirability of ideal conduct in his childhood as well as in youth. When Arnold Mandel asks him about his vocation he reflects, "Doesn't everyone know I am now the most moral man in all of New York, all pure motives and humane and compassionate ideals? Doesn't he know that what I do for a living is I'm good?"(174). He is shocked to learn that Smolka who is an epitome of immorality in his eyes is a professor in Princeton University. According to his moral standards Smolka and Mandel, the "two bad boys", should be "in jail – or the gutter" for their immoral behavior (176). On the other hand, he feels satisfied at the fate of Bubbles Girardi who has been deservedly murdered in a bar.

In fact, the root cause of his guilt and the resultant mental torments is his high ethical ideals. In the tragedy of Portnoy the tragic flaw is his conviction of the desirability of good and his pathetic failure to achieve it. The temptation of hedonistic pleasures is too much for him, and he invariably succumbs to the yearnings of the flesh. He is torn by the conflict between his ethical impulses and his libidinous desires, to use the psychological jargon, between ego and superego. Roth says in *Reading Myself and Others*: "In Portnoy the disapproving moralist who says 'I am horrified' will not disappear when the libidinous slob shows up screaming 'I want!' "[9] It is ironical that his ethical ideals are so lofty and sublime that to attain them seems a Herculean task to him. He himself admits that he is "torn by desires that are repugnant to my conscience, and a conscience repugnant to my desires"(132).

On a deeper level, his moral predicament is similar to that of Christopher Marlowe's hero Dr. Faustus who, while seeing the glimpse of heaven, himself brings about his perdition. Fully conscious of the desirability of good, he perilously and pitifully succumbs to the temptations of evil. Searles also confirms this view when he observes that Portnoy "is intended as a tragic figure."[10] What justifies him in the end is his scorching sense of loss, regret and repentance for the unfulfilled possibilities of his life and his genuine intention to transcend the weakness of the flesh. Naomi, in fact, echoes his own feelings when she contemptuously rejects him saying, "And you are a highly intelligent man – that is what makes it even more disagreeable. The contribution you could make! Such stupid self-deprecation!"(265). The wide gap between his potentialities and his actual achievements, whether he realizes it or not, is one of the major causes of his affliction.

To bring into sharp focus the ethical choices of Portnoy, Roth intentionally selects for him the job of Assistant Commissioner of Human Opportunity for the City of New York which is commensurate with his lofty moral ideals and drastically opposed to his dissolute way of life. It seems ironical that such a morally depraved debauch is entrusted with the noble and philanthropic duty of protecting the rights of the underprivileged and exploited people of society. But it is paradoxically true that he is, on one level, morbidly conscious of his role in his immediate society. Actually, this leads us to one of his major conflicts – between his private life and his role in public life. Emphasizing the social aspect of Portnoy's predicament, McDaniel rightly points out that he is "torn between conflicting loyalties to the public self and the private self."[11] Like Lou Epstein, he is dangling precariously between the expectations of the community and the temptations of physical pleasures. While his sufferings are strikingly similar to those of the typical *schlemiel* found in Jewish fiction – Tommy Wilhelm of *Seize the Day*, Joseph of *Dangling Man* and Frank Alpine of *The Assistant* – Portnoy is never seen to sever his ties with his family and society. Like Paul in *Letting Go*, he is always haunted by a sense of duty towards his family. Comparing Portnoy with Herzog in respect of the affliction of the self outside the orbit of the immediate society, Tony Tanner observes that "at last Roth's interest in the social scene and his feeling for the obsessed self coalesced in the writing."[12]

In the role of a responsible member of the community, Portnoy has a tendency to efface that part of his personality which drags him into the mire of sexual lust, but he is unable to muster up enough strength to overcome his temptations. Tortured by his plight after his encounter with Naomi in Israel, he longs for extinction or conversion into a beast. On various occasions he metaphorically changes his identity; in the hotel in Vermont with Mary Jane Reed, he literally changes his name. This shows his desperate attempt to evade his present situation. Comparing Herzog and Portnoy Tony Tanner remarks:

> In company with most American protagonists of the last decade, their [Herzog's and Portnoy's] main desire is to gain a measure of freedom from the conditioning forces, and some release (even immunity) from those behavioral and intellectual versions of reality which have helped to bring them to their present state of immobility."[13]

What Portnoy so desperately wants to shed comprises mainly the reminiscences of the repressions and inhibitions let loose upon him by his parents in his early childhood and youth. Sophie Portnoy, a stereotypical Jewish mother, forces her authority over her son little bothering about his individual freedom. He is constantly reminded of the exhortations offered by his ineffectual father, a chronic patient of constipation, desperately trying to sell insurance for Boston and Northeastern Life without any prospects of promotion. Jack Portnoy is the typical father figure found in Roth's fiction – civilized, hardworking and self-sacrificing. He works hard to provide for his family what he calls "an umbrella for a rainy day"(7). He cherishes high aspirations for his son and strives to ensure his freedom from the economic and social constrictions he himself has faced in a Gentile society in the postwar America. Portnoy's attitude towards his father is ambivalent. On the one hand, he fully appreciates his father's sacrifices and aspirations for him: "Where he had been imprisoned, I would fly: that was his dream. Mine was its corollary: in my liberation would be his – from ignorance, from exploitation, from anonymity"(8-9). On the other, he feels contempt for "this schmuck, this moron, this Philistine father of mine!"(9). This may be due to the fact that he unconsciously compares his own Jewish culture with the pervasive American culture he has imbibed from the media. .

Portnoy's ethical dilemma is inextricably linked with the moral values traditionally associated with his native Jewish culture. His deep sense of frustration and loss over the plight of his Jewish parents in the materialistic American society dominated by the Gentiles is not much different from that of the typical *schlemiel* found in contemporary Jewish-American fiction. The fear of social and economic insecurity suffered by the Jewish immigrants in the affluent American society seems to have percolated in one form or the other to their offspring and has left an indelible mark on their psyche. In a way, this sense of loss and exploitation may be considered a common heritage of the Jewish immigrants in America. Portnoy laments, "Who filled these parents of mine with such a fearful sense of life? (35). In fact, the victimized and alienated Jew in American society is a recurrent figure in Jewish-American fiction from as early as Isaac Rosenfield's *Passage from Home* and Bellow's The *Victim*. What distinguishes Portnoy from such characters is that instead of being victimized directly by the Gentiles in America he is persecuted by the feelings of repression and guilt induced by his parents (ironically, he suffers defeat and humiliation at the hands of a Jewish girl, Naomi, in Israel – the sanctuary of the Jews).

In his fiction Roth is very much concerned with question of authority over a person's life which will, in turn, determine the degree of personal freedom of the individual in society. He points out in *Reading Myself and Others* that in *Portnoy's Complaint* and *When She Was Good* the protagonists are bent upon opposing the parental authority:

> Though not necessarily 'typical', Alexander Portnoy and Lucy Nelson seem to me, in their extreme resentment and disappointment, like the legendary unhappy children out of two familiar American family myths. In one book it is the Jewish son railing against the seductive mother, in the other the Gentile daughter railing against the alcoholic father.... [14]

The past memories of his childhood with his parents cling to his psyche inextricably. He feels so crippled and unmanned by his parental authority that he cries in pain, "A Jewish man with his parents alive is half the time a helpless infant! ... Spring me from this role I play of the smothered son in the Jewish joke!" (111). In his blurred and distorted vision, he tries to generalize his Jewish predicament and attributes the plight of all the Jewish children to their parents.

> What was it with these Jewish parents — because I am not in this boat alone, oh no, I am on the biggest troop ship afloat ... only look in through the portholes and see us there, stacked to the bulkheads in our bunks, moaning and groaning with such pity for ourselves, the sad and watery-eyed sons of Jewish parents, sick to the gills from rolling through these heavy seas of guilt.... (118)

Because of his confused state of mind, Portnoy sees his troubles as the product of his Jewishness. But Roth, and for that matter the reader, does not have to agree with him. Here he is exaggerating the comic and painful situation of Portnoy to explore the predicament of modern man in moral and social perspectives. In fact, the parallelism in the typical predicament of modern man and that of the Jewish protagonist may be commonly found in the postwar Jewish-American fiction. Mark Shechner refers to this similarity when he says, "The disarray into which the Jewish intellectual was thrown has all the earmarks of a modern dilemma.... [15]

In Portnoy's case, however, his ethnicity is a guiding principle of all his motives and actions. Even in his relationships with women he is mainly guided by his ethnic considerations. Characteristically, the girls he chooses for his lecherous pleasures in America are invariably Gentile and not Jewish. By sleeping with the Gentile girls, he tries, though unsuccessfully, to pacify the gnawing feelings of not belonging to the Gentile majority community of America. Somehow he feels "disenfranchised in a country where a Jew does not fit the media image of an American". [16] For him "America is a *shikse* nestling under your arm whispering love love love love love!"(146). Through sexual intercourse with the Gentile girls he intends to "discover" and "conquer" America (235). The natural corollary of his obsession with the lust of the flesh is that he is incapable of feeling any genuine emotions of love for them. Women are merely objects of physical enjoyment for him. Thereal McCoy is the name he attaches to the idealized version of his adolescent dreams. This imaginary *shikse* indulges with him in all the possible sexual fantasies.

Aside from the sexual pleasures he derives from them, these Gentile girls are totally meaningless for him: so much so that he calls them by fictitious names. Mary Jane Reed, nicknamed by him "The Monkey", is the most suitable girl for the fulfillment of his adolescent sexual fantasies. With a rare abandon, he enjoys all kinds of sexual orgies with this semiliterate, glamorous model. His moral depravity can be seen in "leading her into that triumvirate in Rome" with a whore Lina feeling, at the same time, a sense of guilt and abhorrence for his action (134). Among all of his girls, she at least seems to love him sincerely. But when she expresses her love for him and insists on marriage he cruelly abandons her in a hotel room in Athens. She threatens to commit suicide if he does not marry her, but Portnoy is determined that "I simply cannot, I simply *will* not, enter into a contract to sleep with just one woman for the rest of my days"(104). He metes out the same treatment to Kay Campbell, "The Pumpkin", who was his "girl friend at Antioch"(215). Though he admires her good qualities — "a thoroughly commendable and worthy human being" — he refuses to marry her on the trivial pretext that she does not agree to convert to Judaism (216). With Sarah Abbott, nicknamed by him "The Pilgrim", he is even harsher. He admits frankly that "despite all her many qualities and charms – her devotion, her beauty, her deer like grace, her place in American history – there could never be any 'love' in me for The Pilgrim"(240). In her case at least he articulates his real reasons for not marrying her:

> No, Sally Maulsby was just something nice a son once did for his dad. A little vengeance on Mr. Lindabury for all those nights and Sundays Jack Portnoy spent collecting down in the colored district. A little bonus extracted from Boston & Northeastern, for all those years of service, and exploitation. (240-41)

Portnoy's ethical dilemma is to be seen in the context of his ethnic background. As a result of the clash of his moral values with those of the society, he tries to escape in sexual gratifications, which further blur his vision. He meets his nemesis in Naomi, the sturdy military officer in Israel, who rejects him contemptuously. The myth of Jewishness which he uses as a cover in the Gentile-dominated American society is exploded in Israel where there are few chances of his victimization. And still, he miserably fails to maintain an erection with Naomi in his native land. Though he attributes his impotence to the resemblance between Naomi and his mother, his explanation does not seem to be acceptable. Bettelheim's argument seems to be more plausible when he says that it is "really his oral attachment, his wish to remain the suckling infant forever" which is the cause of his impotence in Israel. [17] Naomi feels pity on his despicable condition and articulates the truth he had been avoiding for such a long time: "You are the most unhappy person I have ever known. You are like a baby"(264). In his utter humiliation at the hands of a Jewish girl, his childhood fears of castration come true and he finds his most potential weapon, his sexuality, to fail him in a land exclusively inhabited by the Jews. Disgustedly and contemptuously, Naomi expresses the reality of his condition, "Mr. Portnoy, you are nothing but a self-hating Jew"(265). In this final hour of revelation, the truth begins to dawn upon him and unable to find his way from his mental maze he desperately seeks the help of his psychoanalyst.

McDaniel is of the opinion that "a central concern of the novel is the absurd state of helplessness, crippledness and victimization in which Portnoy finds himself", but he hastens to add that his present condition is due to "social, communal values that are hypocritical and duplicitous." [18] It would not be gratuitous to affirm that he is a victim of the ethical values of his immediate society which insists on banality and normalcy. Seen in this perspective, the novel appears to be a study in guilt and persecution in the tradition of Kafka and Dostoevsky. Roth himself admits in *Reading Myself and Others* that at the time when he was planning *Portnoy's Complaint* he was "teaching a lot of Kafka" at the University of Pennsylvania.[19] "It was all so funny", he says, "this morbid preoccupation with punishment and guilt. Hideous, but funny." [20] Owing to his moral conflict Portnoy suffers terrible mental pain. Like *When She Was Good*, *Portnoy's Complaint* borders on tragedy though here the medium chosen by Roth is comic. The critics who have been praising the novel only for its humor and fun to the exclusion of its vital and serious issues are oblivious to the real intentions of the writer. In the manner of the great masters of guilt and persecution

Kafka and Dostoevsky, he presents his protagonist in the suffocating labyrinth of guilt and fear of retribution searching desperately for any redeeming light. Instead of finding any solace and salvation he plunges into the mire of sexual excesses which further enhances his despondency. Repressed by his parents from his early childhood, he asserts his manliness in masturbation which brings about in him a horrifying dread of revelation and retribution. He confesses, "I am the Raskolnikov of jerking off – the sticky evidence is everywhere!"(20). When his mother remarks that Hannah has told her about what he has been doing in bathroom he at once reaches the conclusion, "She's missed the underpants! *I've been caught*! Oh, *let* me be dead! I'd just as soon!"(23).

Of course the main source of Portnoy's guilt, in his own opinion, seems to be his ethnicity. In his family everything is clearly divided between what is Jewish and what is *goyische*: "If it's bad it's the *goyim*, if it's good it's the Jews!"(75). This hypocritical and misconceived association of goodness with ethnicity is the source of his moral confusion and misconceptions. His parents remind him "three times a day that life is boundaries and restrictions if it's anything."(79). Quite naturally, he envies the Gentile boys for the freedom they seem to enjoy in the matters of food and sex. He is filled with pity on the sad plight of his Jewish parents when he compares them with the Gentile "grammatical fathers and the composed mothers and the self-assured brothers who all live with them in harmony and bliss behind their *goyische* curtains"(147). He laments in agony: "What have they done for me all their lives, but sacrifice?"(25). When he leaves for Vermont his father cautions him, "DON'T RUN FIRST THING TO A BLONDIE, PLEASE! BECAUSE SHE'LL TAKE YOU FOR ALL YOU'RE WORTH AND THEN LEAVE YOU BLEEDING IN THE GUTTER!"(189). Such admonitions and repressions constitute the weight of the dead past which he wishes to shed from his mind, and he cries in exasperation:

> Spring me from this role I play of the smothered son in the Jewish joke! Because it's beginning to pall a little, at thirty-three! And also it *hoits*, you know, there is *pain* involved, a little human suffering is being felt.... (111)

But the book is, obviously, more than the suffering of a Jewish boy. Portnoy himself is aware of the universality of his predicament. That is exactly why he vehemently insists on his essential humanity before Dr. Spielvogel, "I happen also to be a human being!" (76). Thus it can be safely concluded that Portnoy's predicament transcends the narrow boundaries of ethnicity and assumes a universal dimension. His cry of pain at his helplessness is genuine: "How have I come to be such an enemy and flayer of myself? And so alone! *Oh*, so alone! Nothing but *self*! Locked up in *me*!"(248). This might be the voice of any hero of modern fiction crying in anguish over his alienation and isolation. In fact, one of the dominant features of the contemporary literature is a sense of helplessness and victimization felt by the individual amidst the existential forces. In this way, Jewish-American fiction, broadly speaking, describes the universal predicament of man. In *Reading Myself and Others*, Roth says of Malamud, "What it is to be human, and to be humane, is his deepest concern."[21] The statement applies to his own fiction also. Through his desires and sufferings, Portnoy is actually expressing the aspirations and frustrations of the common humanity.

Under the intolerable burden of his past, there are a few situations which provide a sense of pure harmonious joy to Portnoy. One such occasion is when he plays centre field for a softball team and the other is when he goes with his father to the Turkish baths which he significantly describes as a "place without goyim and women"(49).

Barring such scattered experiences of pure happiness in his childhood, Portnoy lives a life of sensual gratification and guilt. His gnawing sense of guilt induces in him a morbid desire to take revenge on the Gentiles, and for lack of a better weapon he uses his male sexuality to spoil the *shikses* deriving a perverse pleasure and satisfaction. On several occasions, he gives vent to his desire to escape his wretched and disintegrated life, "to be Good, Responsible, & Dutiful to a family of his own"(153). Fed up with his wretched condition, he sometimes plays with the idea of running off to a new place to reform his life like Henry Zuckerman of *The Counterlife,* who flees to Israel to start a new life.

In his moral and psychological crippledness, Portnoy is unable to act decisively in accordance with his ethical tenets. His humanistic ideals dominate his baser and carnal desires and that is precisely the reason that to regain wholesomeness and spiritual vigor he is on the couch of Dr. Spielvogel. His earnest and passionate entreaties testify his wish to be emancipated:

> Oh my secrets, my shame, my palpitations, my flushes, my sweats! The way I respond to the simple vicissitudes of human life! Doctor, I can't stand any more being frightened like this over nothing! Bless me with manhood! Make me brave! Make me strong! Make me *whole*! (37)

He wishes for strength so that he can overcome his temptations for sensual lust and lead a virtuous life.

In fact, a certain kind of dualism can be discerned in Portnoy's attitude towards his condition whether it is viewed from psychological, social or moral perspective. What lies at the core of his problem is that he finds it difficult to wriggle out of his torturing conflict. His aim is to be good but he wants to enjoy his badness. Commenting on the predicament of David Kepesh (of *The*

Breast) and Portnoy, Roth says in *Reading Myself and Others*:

> Speaking broadly, it's the struggle to accommodate warring (or, at least, contending) impulses and desires, to negotiate some kind of inner peace or balance of power, or perhaps just to maintain hostilities at a low destructive level, between the ethical and social yearnings and the implacable, singular lusts for the flesh and its pleasures. The measured self vs. the insatiable self. The accommodating self vs. the ravenous self."[22]

A similar kind of ambivalence is found in Portnoy's attitude towards his father, mother and women in general. He himself admits, though, that due to his Oedipal attachment with his mother he fails to maintain wholesome and lasting relationships with the women he manages to seduce (This is not surprising given his IQ of 158 and his familiarity with the works of such great men of letters as Freud, Keats, Miller and Dostoevsky). Sanford Pinsker rightly compares the book to D.H. Lawrence's *Sons and Lovers* in this respect and asserts that like Paul Morel, Portnoy suffers from Oedipal complex. On one occasion, he virtually imagines being caught red-handed by his father in an objectionable posture with his mother. As far as his relations with other women are concerned, he fails to advance beyond his sensual pleasures and unhesitatingly displays a deep-rooted contempt and cynicism for them. Naomi, at least, has the courage to reveal the truth in his face:

> The way you disapprove of your life! ... You seem to take some special pleasure, some pride, in making yourself the butt of your own peculiar sense of humor. I don't believe you actually want to improve your life. (264)

The last stage of his amorous career displays his abysmal degradation. He reflects, "Maybe the wisest solution for me is to live on all fours!"(270). Thus, instead of achieving his lofty moral ideals he has reduced himself to the level of a beast. At the same time this is his final hour of revelation of the truth about himself. In his last howl of pain there appears some hope of affirmation and regeneration as is shown by Dr. Spielvogel's punch line, "Now vee may perhaps to begin"(274). The word 'begin' itself suggests a new beginning in Portnoy's life.

Portnoy's Complaint, perhaps more than any other novel of Roth, demonstrates his comic genius. The humorous effect seems more pronounced here, since the novel was published after such serious and somber books as *Letting Go* and *When She Was Good*. Nevertheless, as Jay L. Halio pertinently suggests, "Moral imperatives, such as those found in *Letting Go* or *When She Was Good*, are not abandoned in this novel; on the contrary, they become if anything even more pronounced."[23] Here he presents such outrageous and extravagant situations which seem funny and comic to the reader, albeit not necessarily to the protagonist. Sometimes even Portnoy, like the heroes of Kafka, seems to chuckle at his grotesque predicament, though his is a grim and absurd laughter. He realizes that he is living his life "in the middle of a Jewish joke"(36). In the tradition of his contemporary Jewish-American writers like Bellow and Malamud, Roth presents a typical modern hero who, despite his victimization in the existential society, is capable of laughing at himself though the pain and torture are too apparent to be missed.

Roth's flair for comedy, so successfully exhibited in his later books, first found expression in *Portnoy's Complaint*. But humor in the book is entirely different from that in many of his later short stories and novels. For example, humor in *The Great American Novel* is markedly different from that in *Portnoy's Complaint*. About the former Roth says: "The comedy in *The Great American Novel* exists for the sake of no higher value than comedy itself; the redeeming value is not social or cultural reform, or moral instruction, but comic inventiveness."[24] In *Our Gang* the comedy is qualified by a pungent satire on the misuse of political power. In its sexual fantasy *Portnoy's Complaint* is more akin to *The Breast* where the protagonist is baffled by his metamorphosis into a huge breast. *The Breast*, however, lacks the moral and ethical implications of the protagonist's experience of social reality. In *Portnoy's Complaint*, the comedy is "the means by which the character synthesized and articulated his sense of himself and his predicament."[25] Here Roth has organically synthesized the elements of humor and pain in accordance with his literary tenets. He says in *Reading Myself and Others*: "Sheer Playfulness and Deadly Seriousness are my closest friends...."[26] In a characteristic manner, the pangs of anguish are made to co-exist with uproarious laughter in the narrative, creating what Shechner calls "comically grim" situations.[27]

Portnoy frequently imagines himself in fantastical situations creating humor at the expense of his agonized condition. One instance of his mixing of absurd comedy with pain can be seen when unable to get an erection with Bubbles Girardi he masturbates and ejaculates into his own eyes. His morbid imagination is at once fired and he fancies himself blind going home with a dog and a stick. Even his verbal and linguistic skills are matched with his fancy to evoke laughter in the midst of grim – in his morbid imagination – situations. When the whore in the hotel room in Rome asks in Italian where "the signore" would like her to begin he answers, "The signore wishes her to begin at the beginning..."(137). Similarly, he describes to his psychoanalyst the sight of "a fellow-addict fifty years my senior ... dropping his load in his hat"(132). Portnoy recognizes the comic aspect of his situation even as he struggles to free himself from it. The wide gap between his high ethical ideals and the present grotesque condition evokes an awkward kind of laughter which might be the result of his psychological strategy to offset the pain or to tolerate it with more ease. Halio rightly observes: "Portnoy's fantasies reveal the fear underlying his adventuresomeness."[28] The dread of catching syphilis from Bubbles Girardi conjures up before him the ghastly and funny sight of his penis lying on the floor and his parents calling the "Humane Society" as if he were "a rabies *dog*" (167). Portnoy has a penchant for articulating his fears and anguish through the witty and absurd use of language as if he hopes to be free of them through his linguistic skill. As often as not the dread of public exposure of his profligacy finds expression through linguistic exaggeration in newspaper headlines: "ASST HUMAN OPP'Y COMMISH FLOGS DUMMY"(175), "JEW SMOTHERS DEB WITH COCK"(240). These serio-comic instances amply demonstrate Roth's proficiency in fusing comic and grave elements to achieve the rare balance of opposites in his fiction.

As already indicated, Roth firmly believes in family and society as the essential matrix for the individual to grow and mature. Despite his sexual degradation and the resultant anguish and pain, Portnoy resists the temptation of plunging in nihilistic and absurd void. But the humor created by his absurd fantasies of sexual pleasure and the consequent guilt and fear seems to alleviate his pain to some extent. Fantasies appear to be such an essential part of his existence that whatever he perceives through them is considered by him as real.

In *Portnoy's Complaint*, Roth has achieved a rare combination of theme and technique. The narrative technique employed by him in this book is as startling and novel as his frank treatment of sexual matters. Roth has used the psychoanalytic setting in his earlier story "Psychoanalytic Special" and has realized its potential and efficacy to portray the innermost yearnings and tensions of the protagonist. "The psychoanalytic monologue", as he calls this technique, further provides him with justifiable opportunity to use a frank and uninhibited language which would have seemed objectionable in any conventional mode of narrative.[29] The technique enabled him to blend organically the fantastical and realistic elements to achieve his artistic purpose. Still, critics like Howe blatantly labeled the novel as "vulgar". [30] Without going into the intricate and confusing distinction between pornographical literature and realistic portrayal of psychological motives and conflicts, suffice it to say that Roth's intentions in *Portnoy's Complaint* are definitely not prurient. The language used by the author to narrate the experiences of the protagonist serves only to lay bare his guilt-ridden and anguished soul. Realizing the difficulty of communication with society, Portnoy gives vent to his mental agony in front of the doctor to save himself. He uses all the means available to him to express his anger and resentment against the inhuman and unmanning social forces around him because of his vehement desire to wriggle out of his grotesquely painful situation. The "'confessional' strategy" employed by Roth in *Portnoy's Complaint* enabled him to present to the reader his protagonist's burden of reality as he sees it and the actuality of his predicament as seen by the reader.[31]

The novel is divided into six sections corresponding to the different phases of Portnoy's life. But instead of following any chronological order in his confessions, Portnoy recalls the various incidents apparently at random, though actually according to a highly complex design devised by the writer. Pinsker praises this narrative skill of Roth by observing that the writer has painstakingly revised and refined his language "until it achieved the illusion of colloquial speech."[32] Ultimately, the novel takes the shape of an uninterrupted and unbroken utterance of a troubled patient who is bent upon unburdening himself of his past "which won't relinquish" him (271). Roth himself emphasizes this aspect of the book when he says in *Reading Myself and Others* that he had to work hard to create "the illusion of intimacy and spontaneity", and that "'naturalness' happens not to grow on trees."[33] It can be safely concluded that in no other novel has Roth been able to blend his narrative technique and subject matter so harmoniously and organically as in *Portnoy's Complaint*.

The tremendous success of the novel may be ascribed to the universality of its theme. The novel deals with the basic conflict between good and evil in human soul though in the context of a highly materialistic society of postwar era. Portnoy enacts the drama of common man with common aspirations and frailties. He is torn apart by his hedonistic impulses on the one hand and his wish to attain the sublime humane ideals on the other. What intensifies his dilemma is his reluctance to compromise with the normative values imposed on him by the society. His ethical ideals definitely incapacitate him from reaching any reconciliation with the outer forces of banality and normalcy. The ethnic element serves only to reinforce the feelings of claustrophobic suffocation and helplessness caused by the limitations imposed upon his psyche yearning for freedom and self-fulfillment. Portnoy's faith in his ethical ideals is firm and immovable. He may be the victim of his family, community and the larger society or his own baser instincts, yet he does not compromise with his basic human values. In his exploration of social reality, Roth is mainly concerned with those humanitarian values which originate in the heart and are not based upon any artificial and hypothetical moral principles.

Portnoy's acute awareness of his 'sins' is a measurement of his humanitarianism. Though his conflict remains unresolved at the end of the book and he fails deplorably to achieve integration of personality, he justifies himself by his desperate wish to attain his cherished ideals. As the punch line of Dr. Spielvogel shows, he has ample hope of Portnoy's recovery. Portnoy's last cry of pain itself testifies his affirmation of faith in the potentialities of man amidst the adverse forces of social reality. Though Portnoy does not succeed in achieving his ideals, he has entered into the process of resolving the conflict between the opposing impulses of base desires and noble aims and thereby achieving peace and harmony.

REFERENCES

1. Irving Howe, "Philip Roth Reconsidered", *Commentary* (Dec. 1972). Rpt. in *Critical Essays on Philip Roth*, ed. Sanford Pinsker (Boston: Hall, 1982) 243.
2. Bernard F. Rodgers, Jr., *Philip Roth* (Boston: Twayne, 1978) 88.
3. Philip Roth, *Reading Myself and Others* (New York: Farrar, 1975) 33.
4. John N. McDaniel, *The Fiction of Philip Roth* (Haddonfield, NJ: Haddonfield, 1974) 136.
5. George J. Searles, *The Fiction of Philip Roth and John Updike* (Carbondale: Southern Illinois UP, 1985) 19.
6. Bruno Bettelheim, "Portnoy Psychoanalyzed", *Midstream* 15 (June-July 1969). Rpt.in *Philip Roth*, ed. Harold Bloom (New York: Chelsea, 1986) 34.
7. Philip Roth, *Portnoy's Complaint* (London: Jonathan Cape, 1969) 3. All subsequent citations will be to the text as given in this edition and the page numbers will be indicated in parentheses appearing immediately after the quotation.
8. Roth, *Reading Myself* 33.
9. Roth, *Reading Myself* 243.
10. Searles 14.
11. McDaniel 133.

12. Tony Tanner, City *of Words: American Fiction 1950-1970* (New York: Harper, 1971) 313.
13. Tanner 297.
14. Roth, *Reading Myself* 26.
15. Mark Shechner, "Jewish Writers", *Harvard Guide to Contemporary American Writing*, ed. Daniel Hoffman (Delhi: Oxford UP, 1981) 198.
16. Judith Paterson Jones and Guinevera A. Nance, *Philip Roth* (New York: Ungar, 1981) 78.
17. Bettelheim 33.
18. McDaniel 143.
19. Roth, *Reading Myself* 21.
20. Roth, *Reading Myself* 22.
21. Roth, *Reading Myself* 127.
22. Roth, *Reading Myself* 70.
23. Jay L. Halio, *Philip Roth Revisited* (New York: Twayne, 1992) 68.
24. Roth, *Reading Myself* 76.
25. Roth, *Reading Myself* 75.
26. Roth, *Reading Myself* 111.
27. Shechner 236.
28. Halio 71.
29. Roth, *Reading Myself* 41.
30. Howe 244.
31. Roth, *Reading Myself* 99.
32. Sanford Pinsker, *The Comedy that 'Hoits': An Essay on the Fiction of Philip Roth* (Columbia: U of Missouri P, 1975) 58.
33. Roth, *Reading Myself* 219.

6

Reconciliation : *The Professor of Desire*

The Professor of Desire, published in 1977, is generally considered to be the most mature and accomplished book written by Philip Roth. Owing to the universality of its theme and flawless structure, the book has received highly favorable acclaim from the critics. According to George J. Searles, "*The Professor of Desire* is one of Roth's best books because it is among his most intelligent."[1] Similarly, Bernard F. Rodgers, Jr. calls it "the most formal of Roth's fictions."[2] Here, Roth seems to be at his best as far as his style, diction and narrative techniques are concerned. In its subdued and solemn tone, human sympathy and tenderness, and a deep sense of pathos and acceptance of life, it is only matched by his autobiographical book *Patrimony*.

If we accept Martin Amis's classification of Roth's novels in trilogies, *The Professor of Desire* is the last novel of the confessional "Trilogy of Desire."[3] In *The Professor of Desire* as in other two novels of this trilogy, *Portnoy's Complaint* and *My Life as a Man*, the protagonist is afflicted with the conflict between his high ethical ideals and base desires. It is in *The Professor of Desire* that after a painful struggle, he is able to understand his true nature, reconcile the conflicting impulses in his personality and, eventually, attain spiritual harmony and peace.

Neil in *Goodbye, Columbus* is a naive and ideal young man who hesitantly embarks upon his encounter with the social forces in quest of his identity and self-fulfillment. Gabe in *Letting Go* resolves to confront these forces through interpersonal relationships determined, at the same time, to preserve his personal freedom and moral integrity. In Gabe's case, however, his struggle inadvertently leads him to a confused state of mind, as the values by which he sets so much store are found to be discordant to the demands of his social milieu. The protagonist of *When She Was Good* asserts her value system rather self-righteously, and even violently. Thwarted by the forces antagonistic to the individual, she fails to achieve reconciliation and harmony and, ultimately, destroys herself. Roth certainly does not approve of any kind of escape from social reality, howsoever indifferent, or even hostile it may be to the individual's demands and yearnings. In *Portnoy's Complaint*, Portnoy's struggle is as much with the society as with himself. On the one hand, he is at odds with the social forces represented by his Jewish parents and on the other, he is torn by the conflict between the two sides of his own personality.

In *The Professor of Desire,* Roth takes the problem of moral conflict to its logical end. Here, the conflict is almost exclusively internal, albeit always in the ambience of family and society. After enjoying unbridled sexual pleasures, David Kepesh (most of the characters of *The Breast* are recast in *The Professor of Desire*) suffers the pangs of guilt and repentance due to his high moral ideals. After much pain and suffering, he begins to understand his true nature and his condition *vis-à-vis* the social and moral forces governing his existence and arrives at the conclusion that his idealistic notions can coexist with the surrounding pragmatic reality only after some adjustments and modifications on his part. In connection with the fate of the protagonists of *Letting Go, Portnoy's Complaint* and *The Breast*, Roth observes in *Reading Myself and Others* (published before *The Professor of Desire*):

> I can even think of these characters – Gabe Wallach, Alexander Portnoy, and David Kepesh [of *The Breast*]– as three stages of a single explosive projectile that is fired into the barrier that forms one boundary of the individual's identity and experience: that barrier of personal inhibition, ethical conviction and plain, old monumental fear beyond which lies the moral and psychological unknown. Gabe Wallach crashes up against the wall and collapses; Portnoy proceeds on through the fractured mortar, only to become lodged there, half in, half out. It remains for Kepesh to pass right on through the bloodied hole, and out the other end, into no-man's land.[4]

The metaphor aptly describes the ethical fate of his earlier protagonists and can be appropriately extended to the hero of *The Professor of Desire*, since it defines his moral predicament accurately. It can be safely presumed that even after crashing against the wall of moral boundary and suffering the pain, he is able to muster enough strength to survive and with the full knowledge and experience of moral dangers inherent in the process.

Comparing Kepesh's situation to that of Portnoy's, Judith Paterson Jones and Guinevera A. Nance observe that like the latter he "fights a recurring battle between passion and reason, pleasure and duty, violent self-assertion and dedication to the discipline of his profession as a teacher and scholar."[5] But in *Portnoy's Complaint*, the conflict is also external as the hero attributes his suppression and unhappiness to his Jewish parents. Even till the closing lines of the novel Portnoy is not able to resolve his conflicts. Kepesh, on the other hand, "begins to gain some insight into his own internal struggle."[6] And once he realizes the real cause of his conflict, he resolutely wages a war against his libidinous instincts and triumphs in the end, though tentatively. In *The Professor of Desire*, the hero is ultimately able to overcome the adverse forces – mainly internal in his case – and achieves self-fulfillment; albeit like all other things in human life his happiness is tentative and not absolute. Jones and Nance accurately describe the moral progress of Kepesh when they observe: "Kepesh becomes the first of Roth's protagonists to make the transition from professor-rake to 'conscientious' professor."[7]

David Kepesh, the professor of comparative literature, faces the age-old conflict between the base desires of the flesh and high moral ideals, "between reckless erotic ambitions and conscientious intellectual dedication."[8] Early in the novel as a student, Kepesh realizes that like Lord Byron he wants to be "studious by day, dissolute by night" and like Richard Steele imagines himself to be a "rake among scholars, a scholar among rakes."[9] On the one hand, he is the high priest of ethical principles supposed to inspire his students with supreme moral values and on the other cherishes the fulfillment of his most wild erotic desires. Like Portnoy, he suffers the dichotomy of his libidinous urge and conscience. In his early youth, though, he finds it difficult to reconcile these conflicting demands: "Either I turned against my flesh, or it turned against me..." (171). No doubt, unlike Portnoy his childhood is comparatively innocent and happy at the Hungarian Royale, his parents' hotel in the Catskills. Still, the seeds of romantic escapism are present in him from the very beginning which can be discerned in his praise for Herbie Bratasky, his childhood hero, who had the rare gift of mimicking all sorts of sounds. His psychoanalyst rightly remarks: "Moral delinquency has its fascination for you"(102). His tendency to live beyond the moral boundaries is also seen in his unsuccessful attempt to seduce Marcella Walsh in his college days.

However, his lust assumes gigantic proportions in England where he goes as a Fulbright fellow to study Arthurian legends and Icelandic sagas. In London, even before attending his "first lectures on the epic and the romance" he lands in Shepherd Market to find the first whore of his life (28). His voracious indulgence in erotic orgies with the two Swedish girls is reminiscent of Portnoy's sexual adventures with his *shikses*. Elisabeth Elverskog and Birgitta have come to London University to improve their English. Unlike Birgitta, Elisabeth is sensitive and conscientious despite her flair for sexual adventures. Initially, Kepesh feels emotionally attached to her and, as he confesses in his letters to her, romantically fancies marrying her and even having children by her. But after a rather perverse and vigorous sexual workout with Birgitta and Kepesh, Elisabeth feels guilty and repentant and, finally, leaves for Sweden. Birgitta, on the other hand, embodies the true spirit of hedonism and seems to suffer no regret or remorse for her debauchery. In her uninhibited and frank indulgence in sexual pleasures she appears to be a replica of Mary Jane Reed, "The Monkey", of *Portnoy's Complaint*. Her "total immunity from remorse or self-doubt" and her "courteous, respectful and friendly" behavior fascinate Kepesh to her (50). But, finally, Kepesh decides to desert her, for she embodies that side of his moral nature which, ironically, he strongly disapproves. This "perfectly brought-up child of a Stockholm physician and his wife" departs from his life as unobtrusively and gracefully as she plays her role in sexual feats (50).

The first one-third of the novel, where Kepesh is seen to wallow in sensual pleasures, strikingly echoes the atmosphere of *Portnoy's Complaint*. Kepesh resembles Portnoy in his "erotic daredevilry" and the consequent feelings of remorse and guilt (44). After a passionate love making with Birgitta he reflects, "An hour earlier I had been fearful that it might be decades before I was potent again, that my punishment, if such it was, might even last *forever*" (41). The fear of impotence is a natural corollary of the acute pangs of guilt and it again finds expression in his complaint during his session with Dr.Klinger: "I cannot maintain an erection, Dr.Klinger"(103). At this stage, Kepesh does not understand his true nature as he himself admits, "No, nobody understands me, not even I myself"(26). That is precisely the reason why after making the mistake of choosing Birgitta as his paramour, he again decides to marry a woman like Helen Baird despite his awareness of "the deep temperamental divide that has been there from the start" between them (67). However, he faces his characteristic dilemma before taking the plunge:

> Doubting and hoping then, wanting and fearing (anticipating the pleasantest sort of lively future one moment, the worst in the next), I marry Helen Baird – after, that is, nearly three full years devoted to doubting-hoping-wanting-and-fearing."(66)

Nevertheless, he soon discovers that Helen is even worse than Birgitta in the sense that at least the latter was what she appeared and was not afflicted with any psychological dualism. She does enjoy sexual intimacy with Kepesh for some time but leaves him the moment she senses his disinterest in her without so much as a hint of accusation or grumbling. Helen, though beautiful and exotic like her, is driven by a passion for the romantic and the unreal, and certainly does not feel at ease in her role of a domestic married woman.

Kepesh's life with Helen is far from contented, since in his choice of her he has been solely guided by his prurient instincts. Soon after their marriage "mutual criticism and disapproval continue to poison our lives", and he realizes with dismay that Helen is irresistibly drawn to those hollow values which lead nowhere but to moral vacuity (67). The exotic world of romance and fun she enjoyed with Jimmy Metcalf in Hongkong always seems to beckon her like a mirage. In her best make-up, this "princess of the Orient" stealthily visits the airport to be picked up by any stranger and transported to Hongkong or any other Utopia of romance (101). In fact, she does go to Hongkong where she has her experience of evil in the form of her former lover, Metcalf. Characters like Metcalf rarely find a central place in Roth's fictional world as they are on the extreme margin of his ethical spectrum. That is why Metcalf himself is never shown physically in the narrative, and his presence is suggested only indirectly. Mauled physically and psychologically, Helen is brought back from Hongkong by Kepesh himself. But even after her marriage with robust and pragmatic Lowery, she finds life monotonous and boring as she is still lured by her romantic and illusory dreams.

Kepesh's separation from Helen again leaves him in a psychological and moral vacuum. In this transitional stage, "fastened to no one and to nothing, drifting, drifting, sometimes, frighteningly, sinking," he attempts to reorganize his life (103). Like Tarnopol, Zuckerman and Portnoy, he seeks the help of a psychoanalyst, Dr. Frederick Klinger. On his visit to his son in New York, Abe Kepesh is rather disturbed to see the kind of life he is living. At this stage, he is in the abyss of his circumstances; he is having his sessions with his psychoanalyst, he is on anti-depressants, and even in his father's presence an unknown homosexual pesters him with his phone calls at midnight. During this period, he makes friendship with one of his faculty colleagues, Ralph Baumgarten, and both of them try to seduce a girl who, ironically turns out to be Dr.Klinger's daughter. Meanwhile, he gets a job offer from Arthur Schonbrunn, the chairman of the comparative literature program at the State University of New York. Now he makes a serious attempt to understand his motives and intentions in the context of his ethical convictions and the demands of his surrounding society. His confession to Dr. Klinger, "I can't go *ahead*", actually proves his intention to wade through the state of stasis and limbo in which he now finds himself (100). At this moment, his receptivity for truth and will for moral regeneration is at its peak, and gradually reality begins to dawn upon him.

At this crucial stage of his life, Kepesh meets Claire Ovington. In sharp contrast to Helen and Birgitta, she represents positive and affirmative traits of character; unlike them she is pragmatic, mature, self-controlled and considerate. "She is to steadiness", he tells Dr.Klinger, "what Helen was to impetuosity. She is to common sense what Birgitta was to indiscretion"(158). With her help and co-operation, Kepesh starts recuperating from his past psychic wounds and makes serious attempt to reaffirm his faith in himself and the ethical ideals which he cherishes.

In a way, Kepesh's moral development follows the archetypal pattern of innocent bliss to experience and pain which is, ultimately, succeeded by serene, though not unqualified, happiness. Eventually, he arrives at the Chekhovian conclusion about the essential human condition as expressed by one of his students, Kathie Steiner, in her paper:" We are born innocent, we suffer terrible disillusionment before we can gain knowledge, and then we fear death – and we are granted only fragmentary happiness to offset the pain."(94). After his horrid experiences, Kepesh realizes that the moral virtues like renunciation, self-control and stoicism are essential to achieve peace and harmony in life. Commenting on Roth's concerns in *The Professor of Desire,* Jones and Nance say: "He is writing about the human condition – the transformations from innocence to experience, from idealism to disillusionment – and those fragmentary moments of happiness which offset the pain."[10]

The major characters in *The Professor of Desire* seem to fall broadly in two categories which represent two extreme poles of moral alternatives. Kepesh occupies a pivotal position in this moral pattern and he partakes of the characteristics of both the types; in fact, their diverse attributes correspond to the ethical dualism in his own nature. Roth seems to contrast these characters deliberately to bring into sharp focus the moral stance of David Kepesh. The first group consists of such characters as Birgitta, Helen and Baumgarten; whereas Claire, Abe, Professor Soska, Barbatnik, and Schonbrunn fall in the second category. In the early stage of his moral development, Kepesh aligns himself with those belonging to the former feeling, at the same time, an inherent affinity with those of the second category. In fact, the progress of the narrative in the novel corresponds to the gradual but definite moral transformation of Kepesh from the first category to the second one.

This is not to suggest that Roth has any intention of grouping his characters into watertight compartments of good and bad. Far from being moral types, his characters are "round", to use E.M. Forster's term.[11] Occasionally, even such a responsible and upright person as Schonbrunn is found to suffer from moral lapse, as is seen in his attempt to seduce Helen in Kepesh's absence (Helen herself reveals this fact to Kepesh after her marriage with Lowery).

Baumgarten, like Helen and Birgitta, believes in unbridled enjoyment of immoral pleasures. He is not daunted by either the reproach of his social circle or the voice of his conscience in his sexual pursuits. In a sense, he is Kepesh's alter ego inasmuch as he represents the dissolute side of his personality. Kepesh would have liked to tread in his footsteps if he had no moral ideals. Baumgarten's total disillusionment with social and moral values is reflected in his candid and cynical declaration to

Kepesh: "But virtue isn't my bag" (138). But at the same time he voices Kepesh's dislike and reprobation of hypocrisy when he expresses his disgust with moral dissolution of the people like the "esteemed professor" who claim to be the guardian of ethical values in society (139).

In many of Roth's novels, the protagonist is more or less antagonistic to his parents inasmuch as he considers them a kind of hindrance in his quest for personal freedom and self-fulfillment. Zuckerman, Portnoy, Paul, and Lucy are all at loggerheads with their parents. Even in *Goodbye, Columbus,* Aunt Gladys, though caring and affectionate, does not seem to approve of Neil's involvement with the Patimkins owing to their higher social and economic status. In sharp contrast to these characters, Kepesh enjoys a tender and affectionate relationship with both his mother and father. "More than in any other of Roth's novels", Searles observes, "the bittersweet complications of deeply-felt filial love are fully explored, as Kepesh reveals his sincere and unashamed attachment to his parents."[12] He is particularly proud of his mother, who is shown to be an affectionate, orderly and assiduous woman. He remembers with fondness and longing her teaching him to type in their deserted and snow-covered Catskills resort. In the character of Belle Kepesh, there is not the slightest suggestion of the authority and oppression of a Sophie Portnoy, the archetypal Jewish mother in *Portnoy's Complaint*. On their visit to Kepesh in New York, she brings for him packages of food with "DAVID" typed "exactly at the center and underlined in red"(106). With rare compassion and pathos, Roth describes Kepesh's parental affection when he nostalgically recalls his childhood days and longs for sleeping in bed with them. Like the lover in Robert Browning's poem "The Last Ride Together", he tries in vain to turn the present moment of his bliss into eternity.[13]

He exclaims: "And before she dies, we will all hold each other through one last night and morning"(111). Until now, he has not been able to grasp and accept the essential transience and imperfection of life.

His father, Abe Kepesh, embodies all the qualities of the typical father generally found in Roth's fiction. Like his counterparts in *Portnoy's Complaint, Letting Go* and *Patrimony,* he is a hardworking, self-sacrificing and pragmatic person, who "has never said die" in his life (115). Kepesh and his father enjoy a mutually congenial and satisfying relationship. His reverence and love for his father is evidently clear in his profuse praise for him: "Is there a man alive, I wonder, who has led a more exemplary life? Is there an ounce of anything that he has withheld in the performance of his duties?" (245). Abe Kepesh's affection and concern for his son is reflected in his gift of the Shakespeare medallions for him. In its treatment of father-son relationship, *The Professor of Desire* is apparently a precursor of Roth's autobiographical book *Patrimony* in which he describes in detail his own relationship with his father.

On his visit to his son in New York after the latter's divorce from Helen, Abe Kepesh finds his life in the doldrums. He strongly reprehends this kind of living and gives his judgment in clear and unambiguous terms: "All this is all *wrong,* son. It is no way to live!"(114). Mature, wise and pragmatic, he nurses no illusion of escape from the harsh realities of this world and is equipped with the traditional wisdom and moral values to grapple with the hardships of survival. He is shocked to learn that Kepesh has been consulting a psychoanalyst in order to solve his personal problems. His exhortations to his son reflect his firm faith in his inherent social and moral values: "Why not a *wife* to talk to? That's what a wife is for!"(114). Though after the death of Belle Kepesh he is utterly alone, he does not bother his son with his request for company or emotional support like, for example, Gabe's father in *Letting Go*. Quite naturally, he feels childlike excitement and euphoria when he sees his son finally settle down with Claire Ovington.

Mr. Barbatnik, on the other hand, is a father figure like E.I. Lonoff in *The Ghost Writer* and Mr. Patimkin in *Goodbye, Columbus*. His composed and contented conversation with the Kepeshes conjures up a warm and compassionate scene in some nineteenth-century British novel. Although he has had his share of pain and suffering in life, he is at peace with himself and the world without the least trace of regret or grumbling and is rather proud of his horrid struggle to survive the concentration camps. In response to Kepesh's question what he wanted to become before the war started, he replies in his characteristically calm manner: "A human being, someone that could see and understand how we lived, and what was real, and not to flatter myself with lies.... To believe in what doesn't exist, no, that wasn't for me"(257). In a way, his assertion sums up the whole point of the narrative which is also expressed in Kepesh's essay on Chekhov's fiction entitled "Man in a Shell" in which he writes of "license and restraint in Chekhov's world – longings fulfilled, pleasures denied, and the pain occasioned by both"(157). The temperament and character of these father figures reflect and reinforce the ethical convictions of the protagonist who is striving to extricate himself from his moral conflict and achieve spiritual harmony.

Martin Green is of the opinion that "Roth is unusually susceptible to literary influence" in his fiction.[14] Whereas the main characters of *Letting Go* are seen to be under the influence of Henry James, Kepesh in *The Professor of Desire* is under the spell of Kafka and Chekhov besides his mention of the names of such literary masters as Flaubert, Dostoevsky, Browning and Tolstoy. Literature for him is referential as it is for Tarnopol in *My Life as a Man,* who is firmly convinced that literature would help him out from his painful dilemma. Roth has a special fascination for Kafka, as is evident in his innumerable references to him in his fiction. Kafka even appears as a character in his essay-story "Looking at Kafka." *The Breast* seems to be closely patterned on "Metamorphosis" in its absurdist mode, portraying the literal metamorphosis of the hero into a huge breast. The writers who most fascinate Roth are generally found to be those who show a high moral consciousness in their fiction.

During their tour of Europe, Kepesh and Claire visit Kafka's grave in Prague. In his discourse with Soska, the dismissed Czech professor, he discusses the sad plight of the intelligentsia in his country amidst the contemporary political reality. Soska's remark that many of them "survive almost solely on Kafka" holds to be true literally as well as metaphorically in the context of his struggle for survival in his own country after the Russian invasion (169). Here Kafka symbolizes the suffering and victimization of the individual by the social and his own inner forces. Kepesh himself feels in unison with Kafka's characters in his moral crippledness.

However, Anton Chekhov in this novel ceases to be just an 'influence'; he is very much a "part of the subject matter."[15] As Kepesh realizes in the course of his moral regeneration, the characters in Chekhov's fiction make a futile attempt to escape from the humdrum and monotonous life into a romantic world of liberty and adventure, which almost invariably ends in disillusionment and despondency. Kepesh is especially impressed by his short stories in which the characters who deviate from the moral path, particularly in prurient matters, are eventually confounded by trauma and despair. His attempt to apply the fictional truth to his own predicament (he actually intends to confess to his students the reality of his sexual experiences) obviously shows that he arrives at the same conclusions in the end. Expounding Chekhov's philosophy of life he tells his students about his [Chekhov's] "feel for the disillusioning moment and for those processes wherein actuality seemingly pounces upon even our most harmless illusions, not to mention the grand dreams of fulfillment and adventure"(74).

In his later novels Roth concentrates his energies on other aspects of human experience such as the complex relation of art with the personal life of the artist and his social milieu (*Zuckerman Unbound*); complexities arising out of the transformation of the felt experience into fictional form (*Patrimony, The Facts, Deception*); and the social, ethnic and political implications of fiction (*The Counterlife*). On a minor scale, these problems have been touched upon by Roth in *The Professor of Desire* also. For instance, Professor Soska is a victim of political totalitarianism in his country. Forcibly retired from his job as a university teacher, he is now engaged in a futile translation of *Moby Dick* into Czech. The same fate is meted out to his wife, who was formerly employed as a research scientist and now works as a typist in a meat packing plant. To Kepesh's amazement, Professor Soska keeps up his appearances even in such hostile circumstances. Kepesh's indulgence in profligacy is juxtaposed with the political entrapment of Soska who has been denied intellectual freedom. Roth seems to suggest here that if Soska can tolerate so much tyranny it should not be difficult for Kepesh to defy the authority of his flesh over his spirit. Kepesh himself does not fail to see the parallelism of their respective situations as he confesses to Soska:

> Of course you are the one on intimate terms with totalitarianism – but if you'll permit me, I can only compare the body's utter single-mindedness, its cold indifference and absolute contempt for the well being

of the spirit, to some unyielding, authoritarian regime. (171-72)

The choice before both of them is clear: Soska could have chosen to obey the dictates of the existing political establishment. He preferred to oppose them to keep intact his personal dignity and integrity. Similarly, Kepesh chooses to embrace higher moral virtues which, in his opinion, are essential for self-fulfillment and spiritual harmony.

Baumgarten rakes up the problematic issue of the relevance of art to personal experience on the one hand and to social and moral taboos on the other. Despite having a destitute family background, he is totally opposed to the idea of making use of his personal circumstances in his art. Surprisingly, he is the only character in the novel – except Barbatnik, the concentration camp survivor – who, like Portnoy, is discomfited by his Jewish culture and morality. He feels only contempt and cynicism for the snobbish and hypocritical people who in the name of upholding high social and moral standards serve only to support and strengthen the dehumanizing system. In the closing pages of the book, Roth brings Barbatnik and conjures up the horrors of the concentration camps, thus, suggesting the old-problem of racial bigotry during the Holocaust. It is in his later novels like *The Counterlife* and *Operation Shylock* that he deals with such ethnic and political issues in detail.

In her discussion of female characters in Roth's fiction, Mary Allen complains that most of Roth's female characters lack the virtue of "genuine goodness".[16] In her opinion, Roth's heroine tries to control the male character by "wielding her power in the name of goodness."[17] Her conclusions may be justified to some extent in the case of such female characters as Lucy, Maureen, Mary Jane Reed, Helen and Birgitta, but Claire Ovington is certainly an exception. For Kepesh she is like the Biblical good angel who arrives at the most appropriate time in his life to help him in extricating himself from his ethical wilderness. Nowhere has Roth portrayed a female character in such glorifying terms as in this novel.

After Kepesh's unhappy marital life with Helen, Claire appears to him so orderly, affectionate and good that she assumes symbolic significance for him – the symbol of the possibility of a life on a higher ethical level. Besides being beautiful and charming like Helen, she is an assiduous and practical woman, and passionately helps him in recuperating from his moral and psychological exhaustion. At least in the case of Claire, it seems difficult to accept Mary Allen's contention that Roth "rails at the world because he has never found in it a woman who is both strong and good."[18] To spare Kepesh any inconvenience arising out of his obligation to marry her, she gets an abortion without so much as informing him. She later explains her reasons to Kepesh, "I don't want to make anybody unhappy. I don't want to cause anyone pain" (222).

But hers is not the goodness of a Sophie Portnoy who tends to dominate her son's life or a Mrs. Wallach whose obsession with goodness leads inadvertently to undesired interference in other's personal life. With her encouragement and emotional support, Kepesh gradually starts enjoying his life as a professor and a husband. Obviously, his intimate relationship with Claire is no longer founded merely upon his sensual passion for her, for with the passage of time he finds his "overheated frenzy subsiding into quiet physical affection"(199). Unlike Helen she understands his true nature and extends her whole-hearted co-operation in his moral redemption: "For within a year the job is somehow done, a big check mark beside each life-saving item. I give up the anti-depressants, and no abyss opens beneath me" (153). At long last, he feels hopeful of his deliverance from those entrapments of the flesh which were the root cause of generation of conflict in his psyche. In the last section of the novel, Roth describes with rare felicity and lyrical brilliance his sense of pure joy and spiritual bliss. Out of his deep sense of contentment and happiness Kepesh exclaims:

> Oh, Clarissa, ... it's as though the past can't do me any more harm. I just don't have any more regrets. And my fears are gone, too. And it's all from finding you. I'd thought the god of women, who doles them out to you, had looked down on me and said, 'Impossible to please – the hell with him.' And then he sends me Claire. (178-79)

But living with Claire in this blissful state, he is still nagged by doubts and fears and, perhaps, this is the reason why he procrastinates his marriage with her. The "rake" in him is sometimes fed up with the orderly and down-to-earth Claire, as she singularly lacks the raw and uninhibited sexuality exhibited by Birgitta and Helen (17). His exasperation is obvious when he says, "I see how very easily I could have no use for her. The snapshots. The lists. The mouth that will not.... The curriculum-review committee. Everything"(162). During their tour of Europe, he remembers with longing his sensual pleasures with Birgitta though just for a moment. Before long he feels that "all such yearnings have begun to subside, as left to themselves those yearnings will"(163). True, the lure of carnal orgies in his unconscious mind sometimes crops up in the form of his disinterest in Claire: "How much longer before I've had a bellyful of wholesome innocence – how long before the lovely blandness of a life with Claire begins to cloy, to pall, and I am out there once again, mourning what I've lost and looking for my way! (251). Nevertheless, he has realized now that his sexual indulgence is actually an impediment in the fulfillment of his ethical aspirations and the resultant achievement of spiritual harmony which is his ultimate goal. Having realized this truth, he exerts his utmost will and strength to shed the ghost of his past profligacy and turns a new leaf in his life.

In his Edenic garden Helen enters like a temptress. However, during their brief interaction he does not show the faintest sign of temptation by her physical charms. Far from it, he feels a kind of pity for her: "Only it is Helen's bad luck that she cannot stand him [her husband]. Still Jimmy – still those dreams of what might and should have been, if only moral repugnance had not intervened"(218). Nevertheless, he is certainly perturbed by his psychological fear of the loss of his sexual passion for Claire: "I can't say it, not tonight, but within a year my passion will be dead. Already it is dying and I am afraid that there is nothing I can do to save it"(261). But now that he is in "his middle thirties, having recovered finally from the mistakes of his twenties", he has understood the essential condition of man in this world (259). With determination, self-denial and self-control, he is able to extricate himself from the labyrinth of his illusions and misconceptions, and starts "living at last in accordance with my [his] true spirit"(196). No doubt, there are pitfalls and obstacles in his quest, they are but an inevitable and essential part of life. His choice to act resolutely and with all his inner resources eventually leads him to his destination.

In sharp contrast to the moral haziness prevalent in *Letting Go*, Roth presents the ethical alternatives of the protagonist in a fairly clear perspective in *The Professor of Desire*. In the opening pages of the novel, he portrays Kepesh's innocent and harmonious state of mind during his childhood spent with his parents in their Catskills resort. He enjoys the taintless bliss of childhood totally unaware of the experience of evil and the consequent disillusionment and pain. It is during his Fulbright years, his "Age of Exploration", that he earnestly pursues the fulfillment of his lascivious desires (147). Even in this phase of erotomania, he is acutely aware of his ethical ideals. Deeply influenced by the fiction of Chekhov, he identifies himself with his characters. He seems to feel such "humiliations and failures" as faced by those characters of Chekhov who seek a way *out* of the shell of restrictions and convention, out of the pervasive boredom and the stifling despair, out of the painful marital situations and the endemic social falsity, into what they take to be a vibrant and desirable life. (156)

In the final stage of his ethical evolution, Kepesh accepts the moral boundaries and restrictions within which life has to be lived and decides to make no attempt either to cross or demolish them. Now he is firmly convinced of the supremacy of the salvation of soul over the gratification of the senses. On discovering the fact of Claire's abortion he says: "Is there not a point on life's way when one yields to duty, *welcomes* duty as once one yielded to pleasure, to passion, to adventure – a time when duty is the pleasure, rather than pleasure the duty...."(253)

Some critics are of the opinion that in the end Kepesh gets only "fragmentary happiness in a relationship with Claire Ovington."[19] According to Jones and Nance, Kepesh's statement that in his relationship with Claire he feels "sealed up into something wonderful"(164) amply demonstrates that he considers his life with Claire as "entrapment."[20] But Kepesh has now learnt to preserve the sanctity of the social and moral bonds which are an essential part of human life. The word 'wonderful' itself suggests the sense of psychological fulfillment and harmony he feels in his limited life with Claire. Rodgers also complains that "his dream of Kafka's whore makes it clear that the struggle within him has been repressed, not ended."[21] True, in the absurd dream he has the night before leaving Prague, he sees Kafka's whore, Eva, who invites him to touch her withered private parts. But his reluctance to accept her lascivious offer amply shows his disinterest in wayward sexual pleasures. Moreover, his vision of the whore as a decrepit old hag may be interpreted as an evidence of his realization of the futility of carnal gratifications.

Mark Shechner calls *The Professor of Desire* "a novel of convalescence", celebrating the "erotic and emotional recovery" of the protagonist.[22] It would be more appropriate to call it a novel of moral convalescence, as it portrays the process of the hero's deliverance from the turbulence caused by his ethical degeneracy. In the closing pages of the novel, Roth describes with rare felicity Kepesh's domestic joy and happiness:

> It looks and feels to both of them as though they have been saved, and in large part by one another. They are in love. But after dinner by candlelight, one of the old men tells of his life, about the utter ruination of a world, and about the blows that keep on coming. And that's it. The story ends just like this: her pretty head on his shoulder; his hand stroking her hair; their owl hooting; their constellations all in order – their medallions all in order; their guests in their freshly made beds; and their summer cottage, so cozy and inviting, just down the hill from where they sit together wondering about what they have to fear. Music is playing in the house. (260)

The tenderness, sentimental affection, deep serenity and contentment expressed in the passage evoke a scene from a novel of Charles Dickens or George Eliot. It reflects the reconciliation and composure attained by a man who has had the painful experience of divergence from the ethical path approved by his milieu and his own conscience. He appears, eventually, to have extricated himself from the gnawing dilemma of restraint and passion, and achieved spiritual harmony.

Still, it goes without saying that Kepesh is pestered by many doubts and apprehensions though of a different nature. In fact, his discomfiture has much to do with his fear of the possibility of relapse into his former moral degeneration. As far as his promiscuous intentions are concerned, he is fully satisfied with Claire. He says, "Claire is enough. Yes, 'Claire' and 'enough' – they, too, are one word"(165). This shows how far Kepesh has come from his anguished state when he confessed to Dr. Klinger in exasperation, "I should have gone all the way and become Birgitta's pimp"(101). His apprehensions serve only to show that the probability of deviation from one's chosen path cannot be ruled out permanently and man can preserve his moral ideals only by strenuous and constant efforts.

Even in the last paragraph of the novel, Kepesh is seen to be troubled by "bad dreams" sweeping through him "like water through a fish's gills" implying the precariousness of his happiness (262). Roth seems to suggest here that the evil in the form of carnal temptations is always lurking below the outer surface of normalcy and can erupt out any moment. But in the very next line Kepesh reaffirms his faith in his latent capabilities: "Near dawn I awaken to discover that the house is not in ashes nor have I been abandoned in my bed as an incurable. My willing Clarissa is with me still!"(262). After his harrowing moral ordeal Kepesh has, at long last, understood and learnt to accept the essential human condition. His predicament transcends the narrow social boundaries and assumes a universal dimension. There are no permanent solutions and life has to be accepted in its entirety and with all its imperfections. Moreover, as Roth himself emphasizes the point in *Reading Myself and Others*, the artist's job is to present the situation honestly and straightforwardly and not to try to suggest any solution. He says: "Chekhov makes a distinction between 'the solution of the problem and a correct presentation of the problem' – and adds, 'only the latter is obligatory for the artist.'"[23] And Roth has certainly succeeded in achieving his artistic purpose in *The Professor of Desire*.

REFERENCES

1. George J. Searles, *The Fiction of Philip Roth and John Updike* (Carbondale: Southern Illinois UP, 1985) 63.
2. Bernard F. Rodgers, Jr., *Philip Roth* (Boston: Twayne, 1978) 160.
3. Quoted in George J. Searles, *The Fiction of Philip Roth and John Updike,* 166.
4. Roth, *Reading Myself and Others19 75) 85.*
5. Judith Paterson Jones and Guinevera A. Nance, *Philip Roth* (New York: Ungar, 1981) 87.
6. Jones and Nance 116.
7. Jones and Nance 112.
8. Hermione Lee, *Philip Roth* (London: Methuen, 1982) 65.
9. Philip Roth, *The Professor of Desire* (London: Vintage, 1995) 17.

   All subsequent citations will be to the text as given in this edition and the page numbers will be indicated in parentheses appearing immediately after the quotation.
10. Jones and Nance 118.
11. E.M. Forster, *Aspects of the Novel,* ed. Oliver Stallybrass (Harmondsworth: Penguin, 1974) 73.
12. Searles 61.
13. Robert Browning, "The Last Ride Together", *Fifteen Poets* (London: Oxford UP, 1965) 432.
14. Martin Green, Introduction, *A Philip Roth Reader,* by Philip Roth (London: Vintage, 1993) XI.
15. Green XIV.

16. Mary Allen, "When She Was Good She was Horrid", *The Necessary Blankness: Women in Major American Fiction of the Sixties* (Urbana: U of Illinois P, 1976). Rpt. in *Philip Roth*, ed. Harold Bloom (New York: Chelsea, 1986) 146.
17. Allen 125.
18. Allen 147.
19. Jones and Nance 117.
20. Jones and Nance 118.
21. Rodgers 163.
22. Mark Shechner, "Jewish Writers", *Harvard Guide to Contemporary American Writing*, ed. Daniel Hoffman (Delhi: Oxford UP, 1981) 235.
23. Roth, *Reading Myself* 18.

7

Conclusion

After the publication of twenty-odd books, Philip Roth is still actively engaged in creative writing and is exploring new vistas of human experience. His aesthetic and creative energies are far from exhausted and are being utilized to explore yet other aspects of human experience. Among the contemporary American novelists Roth has earned a distinguished place.

This book undertook a detailed examination of five of his novels, namely *Goodbye, Columbus, Letting Go, When She Was Good, Portnoy's Complaint* and *The Professor of Desire*. These novels belong to the early phase of his literary career when Roth's concern with ethical aspect of human experience appears most pronounced in his fiction. In these novels ethical and moral issues underlying individual predicaments and conflicts are probed with rare intensity. Roth has attempted to evaluate the contemporary relevance of these ethical dimensions with a great aesthetic integrity. Moreover, these novels have a thematic unity and continuity and are written largely in the realistic mode.

Roth is fully aware that the artist should not have an ulterior motive of propagating any moral principles or doctrine. His job is to present the situation truthfully before the reader and suggest the desirability of his willing participation in the moral process going on around him. The essence of his artistic achievement is that in his portrayal of man's search for selfhood, identity and struggle for survival amidst the existential reality he lays special emphasis on the ethical aspect of human experience which has somehow been denied its due significance in recent American fiction. Though literature is not a panacea for all the social and moral problems, it certainly makes us conscious of the need of a set of universally accepted moral values for the smooth functioning of our social and moral institutions. It is neither desirable nor feasible for man to exist in isolation and estrangement apart from his recognizable social world. To preserve the order and sanctity of the human world, some norms of moral conduct are essential if we accept the Platonic conception of the artist as moral guardian of society. And Roth's fiction seems fully to endorse this point of view.

This does not imply that Roth has any intention to impose any prescriptive value system on his readers. In his fiction, the virtues and values are suggested by the narrative itself, through what he. calls "the manner of presentation."[1] His fiction displays his firm belief in those ethical values which inspire the individual to become a better and truer component of his social system and for this purpose he relies more on the potency of the heart as the infallible guide than any prescriptive value system. This is not a mean achievement in the chaos and anarchy of the modern society where man is found to shift his ethical choices frequently under the pressure of the demands of conformity. Roth's insistence on not neglecting the exhortations of the heart adequately serves his artistic purpose which is to expand man's moral consciousness. In this context, he remarks in *Reading Myself and Others*: "And this expansion of moral consciousness, this exploration of moral fantasy, is of considerable value to a man and to society".[2]

Roth has been called a "social realist" by some critics, and like other postwar American writers, he chronicles in his fiction the contemporary historical experience drawing heavily upon his personal experience in the Jewish minority community to which he belongs. [3] Yet, like Bellow, he is totally assimilated Jewish-American writer whose fiction transcends narrow ethnicity and assumes universal significance. His fiction encompasses the vast panorama of human experience with its essential limitations and possibilities.

As far as Roth is concerned, moral values form an integral part of any kind of literary experience. Perhaps, none of his contemporaries is so much concerned about the moral aspect of social reality as Roth. The hero in recent American fiction is seen to assume different moral postures to survive in his society which demands unconditional conformity denying, at the same time, any tangible assurance of self-fulfillment and moral integrity. Not infrequently he attempts to escape into a dark world of fantasy and absurdism. Roth certainly does not approve of the tendency of the individual to escape from the tangible social world. He explores the moral predicament of modern man by making his characters descend into the depth of grotesqueness and ugliness of the social reality. His hero has a firm belief in the possibilities of his growth and rejuvenation only in the matrix of family and society. Instead of recoiling in his own self and casting aside the recognizable social world, the Rothian protagonist makes some adjustments in his own response to the hostile forces which impinge on his psyche from outside and to the demoniacal side of his own nature. In his encounter with the adverse forces, he invariably chooses to be on the positive side of the ethical spectrum. Even in most crucial situations, he neither deviates from his chosen ethical stance nor makes compromise with the forces of negation which are discordant to his own ethical ideals.

Roth is highly conscious of the importance of an effective medium for the modern novelist to express the contemporary reality which, he feels, is absurd, elusive and, even incredible by nature. It is not surprising, therefore, that he has employed successfully diverse kinds of narrative and stylistic devices in his books. He can manipulate his narrative techniques dexterously to tell a tale from different points of view. His diction has amazing flexibility and variety, and he can manoeuvre it to portray any character and his specific milieu. The apparent spontaneity of his narrative is, actually, the outcome of a highly polished and skilful use of diction and syntax. In his adaptable vernacular language, choice of words and manipulation of sentence structure, Searles rightly links him with the native American tradition of such writers as Mark Twain, Gertrude Stein and Ernest Hemingway. In short, Roth is fully aware of the vital connection between the fictional material and the form. Through an appropriate and effective fictional medium, he has successfully probed the modern man's predicament in the contemporary society and conveyed his affirmation in his latent capabilities to overcome the forces of negation and annihilation.

This book undoubtedly has a limited scope as I did not set out to undertake a comprehensive analysis of all of Roth's fiction. Roth is certainly a prolific writer, as is evident from the large number of novels, short stories, critical essays and even a play written by him over a span of more than four decades. Much can be said about the problematic issue of his Jewishness in relation to the secular American society in which he grew up, and much more about his political and social satires. In fact, his fiction offers an interesting range of themes and technical experimentations for further study. Moreover, he is still engaged in creative writing and it is difficult, and even hazardous, to summarize the artistic vision of a living writer in absolute and conclusive terms. The book has merely attempted to critically analyze a few of his early novels to expound the evolution of his ethical vision.

REFERENCES

1 Philip Roth, *Reading Myself and Others* (New York: Farrar, .1975) 27.

2. Roth, *Reading Myself* 151.

3. George J. Searles, *The Fiction of Philip Roth and John Updike* (Carbondale: Southern Illinois UP, 1985) 2.

Bibliography

PRIMARY SOURCES

1. Books

American Pastoral. New York: Vintage, 1998.

The Anatomy Lesson. New York: Farrar, 1981.

The Breast. London: Jonathan Cape, 1973.

The Counterlife. New York: Farrar, 1987.

Deception. New York: Simon & Schuster, 1990.

The Dying Animal. New York: Vintage, 2002.

Everyman. London: Vintage, 2007.

The Facts: A Novelist's Autobiography. New York: Farrar, 1988.

The Ghost Writer. New York: Farrar, 1979.

Goodbye, Columbus and Five Short Stories. Thirtieth Anniversary ed. Boston: Houghton, 1989.

The Great American Novel. London: Vintage, 1991.

The Human Stain. New York: Vintage, 2001.

I Married a Communist. Boston: Houghton, 1998.

Letting Go. London: Corgi, 1964.

My Life as a Man. New York: Holt, 1974.

Operation Shylock. London: Vintage, 1994.

Our Gang. London: Vintage, 1994.

Patrimony: A True Story. London: Vintage, 1992.

A Philip Roth Reader. London: Vintage, 1993.

The Plot Against America. London: Vintage, 2003.

Portnoy's Complaint. London: Jonathan Cape, 1969.

The Prague Orgy. London: Jonathan Cape, 1985.

The Professor of Desire. London: Vintage, 1995.

Reading Myself and Others. New York: Farrar, 1975.

Sabbath's Theater. Boston: Houghton, 1995.

When She Was Good. New York: Bantam, 1968.

Zuckerman Bound. New York: Farrar, 1985.

Zuckerman Unbound. New York: Farrar, 1981.

2. Uncollected Reviews, Essays and Short Stories

"Armando and the Fraud." *Et Cetera* Oct. 1953: 21-32.

"The Box of Truths." *Et Cetera* Oct. 1952: 10-12.

"The Contest for Aaron Gold." *Epoch* 5-6 (1955): 37-51.

"The Day It Snowed." *Chicago Review* 8(1954): 34-45.

"Expect the Vandals." *Esquire* Dec. 1958: 208-28.

"The Fence." *Et Cetera* May 1953: 18-23.

"Heard Melodies are Sweeter." *Esquire* Aug. 1958: 58.

"In Search of Kafka and Other Answers." *The New York Times Book Review* 15 Feb. 1976: 6-7.

"The Kind of Person I Am." *New Yorker* 29 Nov. 1958: 173-178.

"The Mistaken." *American Judaism* 10(1960): 10.

"Novotny's Pain." *New Yorker* Oct. 27, 1962: 46-56.

"On the Air." *New American Review* 10 (1970): 7-49.

"Positive Thinking on Pennsylvania Avenue." *Chicago Review* 11 (1957): 21-24.

"Psychoanalytic Special." *Esquire* Nov. 1963: 106.

"Recollections from Beyond the Last Rope." *Harper's* July 1959: 42-48.

"A Talk with Aharon Appelfeld." *The New York Times Book Review* 28 Feb. 1988: 1.

3. Interviews

"The Ghost of Roth." Interview with Alain Finkielkraut. *Esquire* Sept. 1981: 92-97.

"Jewishness and the Younger Intellectuals." *Commentary* Apr. 1961: 306-59. Symposium.

"Philip Roth: Should Sane Women Shy Away from Him at Parties." Interview with Ronald Hayman. *Sunday Times Magazine* 22 Mar. 1981: 38-42.

"Second Dialogue in Israel." *Congress Bi-Weekly* 16 Sept. 1963: 4-85. Symposium.

"A Visit with Philip Roth." Interview with James Atlas. *The New York Times Book Review* 2 Sept. 1979: 1.

"What Facts? A Talk with Roth." Interview with Jonathan Brent. *The New York Times Book Review* 28 Sept. 1988: 46-47.

SECONDARY SOURCES

1. Books

Allen, Frederick Lewis. *The Big Change*. New York: Harper and Brothers, 1952.

Allen, Walter. *The Modern Novel in Britain and the United States*. New York: Dutton, 1964.

Axthelm, Peter M. *The Modern Confessional Novel*. New Haven: Yale UP, 1967.

Balakian, Nona, and Charles Simmons, eds. *The Creative Present: Notes on Contemporary American Fiction*. Garden City, NY: Doubleday, 1963.

Baumgarten, Murray, and Barbara Gottfried. *Understanding Philip Roth*. Columbia: U of South Carolina P, 1990.

Bellow, Saul. *Seize the Day*. London: Penguin, 1988.

Bergonzi, Bernard. *The Situation of the Novel*. London: Macmillan, 1970.

Bergson, Henri. Laughter: *An Essay on the Meaning of the Comic*. New York: Macmillan, 1937.

Bloom, Harold, ed. *Philip Roth*. New York: Chelsea, 1986.

Bradbury, Malcolm. *The Modern American Novel*. Oxford: Oxford, UP, 1983.

Brinton, Crane. *Ideas and Men: The Story of Western Thought*. Englewood Cliffs, NJ: Prentice Hall, 1963.

Browne, Lewis. *Stranger than Fiction: A Short History of the Jews from Earliest Times to the Present Day*. New York: Macmillan, 1956.

Chase, Richard. *The American Novel and its Tradition*. Garden City, NY: Doubleday, 1957.

Cohen, Sarah Blacher, ed. *Jewish Wry*. Bloomington: Indiana UP, 1987.

Cooper, Alan. *Philip Roth and the Jews*. Albany, NY: State U of New York P, 1996.

Fiedler, Leslie A. *An End to Innocence: Essays on Culture and Politics*. New York: Stein and Day, 1972.

——. *Love and Death in the American Novel*. New York: Stein and Day, 1960.

——. *Waiting for the End: The American Literary Scene from Hemingway to Baldwin*. New York: Stein and Day, 1965.

Finkelstein, Sidney. *Existentialism and Alienation in American Literature*, New York: International, 1965.

Frankena, William K. *Ethics*. New Delhi: Prentice Hall of India, 1982.

Friedman, Alan. *The Turn of the Novel: The Transition to Modern Fiction*. London: Oxford UP, 1966.

Galloway, David. *The Absurd Hero in American Fiction*. Austin: U of Texas P, 1966.

Gardner, John. *On Moral Fiction*. New York: Basic, 1978.

Geismar, Maxwell. *American Moderns: From Rebellion to Conformity*. New York: Hill and Wang, 1958.

Girgus, Sam B. *The New Covenant: Jewish Writers and the American Idea*, Chapel Hill: U of North Carolina P, 1984.

Gittleman, Sol. *From Shtetl to Suburbia: The Family in Jewish Literary Imagination*. Boston: Beacon, 1978.

Goldknopf, David. *The Life of the Novel*. Chicago: U of Chicago P, 1972.

Gordon, Milton M. *Assimilation in American Life: The Role of Race, Religion and National Origins*. New York: Oxford UP, 1964.

Guttmann, Allen. *The Jewish Writer in America: Assimilation and the Crisis of Identity*. New York: Oxford UP, 1971.

Halio, Jay L. *Philip Roth Revisited*. New York: Twayne, 1992.

Hassan, Ihab. *Radical Innocence: Studies in the Contemporary American Novel*. Princeton, NJ: Princeton UP, 1961.

Hendin, Josephine. *Vulnerable People: A View of American Fiction Since 1945*. Delhi: Oxford UP, 1979.

Hicks, Granville. *The Living Novel*. New York: Macmillan, 1957.

Hough, Graham. *Literature and Morals in the Culture of Today*. London: Duckworth, 1963.

Howe, Irving. *The Critical Point: On Literature and Culture*. New York: Horizon Press, 1973.

——. *The Literature of America: Nineteenth Century*. New York: McGraw, 1970.

Jones, Judith Paterson, and Guinevera A. Nance. *Philip Roth*. New York: Ungar, 1981.

Kazin, Alfred, ed. *The American Novel Since World War II*. Greenwich: Fawcett, 1969.

——. *Bright Book of Life: American Novelists and Storytellers from Hemingway to Mailer*. Boston: Little, Brown, 1973.

Klein, Marcus. *After Alienation: American Novel in Mid-Century*. New York: The World, 1964.

Langer, Lawrence L. *The Holocaust and the Literary Imagination*. New Haven: Yale UP, 1975.

Lee, Hermione. *Philip Roth*. London: Methuen, 1982.

Malin, Irving. *Contemporary American – Jewish Literature: Critical Essays*. Bloomington: Indiana UP, 1973.

——. *Jews and Americans*. Illinois: Southern Illinois UP, 1965.

Malinowski, Bronislaw. *A Scientific Theory of Culture*. Chapel: U of North Carolina P, 1944.

McDaniel, John N. *The Fiction of Philip Roth*. Haddonfield, NJ: Haddonfield, 1974.

Meeter, Glenn. *Bernard Malamud and Philip Roth: A Critical Essay*. Grand Rapids, MI: Eerdmans, 1968.

Milbauer, Asher Z., and Donald G. Watson, eds. *Reading Philip Roth*. New York: St. Martin's, 1988.

Muller, Herbert. *Modern Fiction: A Study of Values*. New York: McGraw, 1974.

Olderman, Raymond. *Beyond the Wasteland: A Study of the American Novel in the Nineteen-Sixties*. New Haven: Yale UP, 1972.

Parker, James. *The Jewish Problem in the Modern World*. London: Thornton Butterworth, 1979.

Pinsker, Sanford. *The Comedy That 'Hoits': An Essay on the Fiction of Philip Roth*. Columbia: U of Missouri P, 1975.

——, ed. *Critical Essays on Philip Roth*. Boston: Hall, 1982.

Pizer, Donald. *Twentieth Century American Literary Naturalism: An Interpretation*. Carbondale: Southern Illinois UP, 1982.

Rodgers, Bernard F., Jr. *Philip Roth*. Boston: Twayne, 1978.

——, Comp. *Philip Roth: A Bibliography*. 2nd ed. Metuchen, NJ: Scarecrow, 1984.

Ruland, Richard, and Malcolm Bradbury. *From Puritanism to Postmodernism: A History of American Literature*. New York: Penguin, 1992.

Rupp, Richard H. *Celebration in Postwar American Fiction, 1945-1967*. Coral Cables: U of Miami P, 1970.

Schultz, Max F. *Radical Sophistication: Studies in Contemporary Jewish-American Novelists*. Athens, Ohio: Ohio UP, 1969.

Searles, George J. *The Fiction of Philip Roth and John Updike*. Carbondale: Southern Illinois UP, 1985.

Shechner, Mark. *After the Revolution: Studies in the Contemporary Jewish Imagination*. Bloomington: Indiana UP, 1987.

Solotaroff, Theodore. *The Red-Hot Vacuum*. New York: Atheneum, 1970.

Tanner, Tony. *City of Words: American Fiction 1950-1970*. New York: Harper, 1971.

Trilling, Lionel. *The Liberal Imagination*. Garden City, NY: Doubleday, 1953.

Veatch, Henry B. *Rational Man: A Modern Interpretation of Aristotalian Ethics*. Bloomington: Indiana UP, 1962.

Waldmeir, Joseph J. *Recent American Fiction: Some Critical Views*. Boston: Houghton, 1963.

Warnock, Mary. *Ethics since 1990*. Oxford: Oxford UP, 1978.

Weinberg, Helen. *The New Novel in America: The Kafkan Mode in Contemporary Fiction*. Ithaca: Cornell UP, 1970.

Whitfield, Stephen J. *Voices of Jacob, Hands of Esau: Jews in American Life and Thought*. Hamden, CT: Archon, 1984.

Wisse, Ruth. *The Schlemiel as Modern Hero*. Chicago: U of Chicago P, 1971.

2. Articles

Allen, Mary. "When She Was Good She Was Horrid." *The Necessary Blankness: Women in Major American Fiction of the Sixties*. Urbana: U of Illinois P, 1976. 70-96. Rpt. in *Philip* Roth. Ed. Harold Bloom. New York: Chelsea, 1986. 125-47.

Alter, Robert. "The Education of David Kepesh". *Partisan Review* 46(1979): 478-81.

Appelfeld, Aharon, "The Artist as a Jewish Writer." Trans. Asher Z. Milbauer and Donald G. Watson. *Reading Philip Roth*. Eds. Asher Z. Milbauer and Donald G. Watson. New York: St. Martin's Press, 1988. 13-16.

Ardino, Frank. " 'Hit Sign, Win Suit': Abraham, Isaac, and the Schwabs Living Over the Scoreboard in Roth's *The Great American Novel." Studies in American Jewish Literature* 8 (Fall 1989): 219-23.

Barnes, Julian. "Philip Roth in Israel: *The Counterlife*". *London Review of Books* 5 Mar. 1987: 3-9.

Bettelheim, Bruno. "Portnoy Psychoanalyzed." *Midstream* 15 (June-July 1969): 3-10. Rpt. in Bloom 25-34.

Birkerts, Sven. "Philip Roth." *American Energies: Essays on Fiction*. New York: William Marrow, 1992. 260-65.

Blair, Walter, and Hill Hamlin. *"The Great American Novel"*. *America's Humor: From Poor Richard to Doonesbury*. New York: Oxford UP, 1978. Rpt. in Pinsker 217-28.

Brent, Jonathan. "The Unspeakable Self: Philip Roth and the Imagination." Milbauer and Watson 180-200.

Charney, Maurice. "Sexuality and Self-Fulfilment: *Portnoy's Complaint* and Fear of Flying." *Sexual Fiction*. New York: Methuen, 1981. 113-31.

Cheuse, Alan. "A World Without Realists." *Studies on the Left* 4 (Spring 1964): 68-82.

Cohen, Joseph. "Paradise Lost. Paradise Regained: Reflections on Philip Roth's Recent Fiction." *Studies in American Jewish Literature* 8(Fall 1989): 196-204.

Cohen, Sarah Blacher. "Philip Roth's Would-be Patriarchs and Their Shikses and Shrews." *Studies in American Jewish Literature* 1 (Spring 1975): 16-23. Rpt. in Pinsker 209-16.

Cooper, Alan. "The Jewish Sit-Down Comedy of Philip Roth." *Jewish Wry*. Ed. Sarah Blacher Cohen. Bloomington: Indiana UP, 1987. 158-77.

Cooperman, Stanley. "Philip Roth: 'Old Jacob's Eye' with a Squint." *Twentieth Century Literature* 19 (July 1973): 203-16.

Crews, Frederick. "Uplift." *New York Review of Books* Nov. 16, 1972: 18-20. Rpt. in Pinsker 64-68.

Deer, Irving, and Harriet Deer. "Philip Roth and the Crisis in American Fiction." *Minnesota Review* 6(1966): 353-60.

Denby, David. "The Gripes of Roth." *New Republic* 21 Nov. 1988: 37-40.

Dickstein, Morris. "Black Humor and History: The Early Sixties." *Gates of Eden – American Culture in the Sixties*. New York: Basic, 1977. 91-127.

Donaldson, Scott. "Philip Roth: The Meanings of Letting Go." *Contemporary Literature* 11 (Winter 1970): 21-35.

Eiland, Howard. "Philip Roth: The Ambiguities of Desire." Pinsker 255-65.

Feldman, Irving, "A Sentimental Education Circa 1956." *Commentary* Sept. 1962: 273-76. Rpt. in Pinsker 32-36.

Fiedler, Leslie. "The Image of Newark and the Indignities of Love: Notes on Philip Roth". *Midstream* 5 (Summer 1959): 96-99. Rpt. in Pinsker 23-27.

Forrey, Robert. "Oedipal Politics in *Portnoy's Complaint.*" Pinsker 266-74.

Friedman, Alan Warren. "The Jew's Complaint in Recent American Fiction: Beyond Exodus and Still in the Wilderness." *Southern Review* 8 (Fall 1972): 41-59. Rpt. in Pinsker 149-63.

Gass, William. "The Sporting News." *New York Review of Books* May 31, 1973: 7.

Girgus, Sam B. "Portnoy's Prayer: Philip Roth and the American Unconscious." Milbauer and Watson 126-43.

Gittleman, Sol. "The Pecks of Woodenton, Long Island, Thirty Years Later: Another Look at 'Eli, the Fanatic'." *Studies in American Jewish Literature* 8 (Fall 1989): 138-42.

Goldberg, Mark F. "Books: The Jew as Lover." *National Jewish Monthly* Nov.1969: 64-67.

Gray, Paul. "A Surprising Mid-Life Striptease." *Time* 19 Sept. 1988: 94-95.

Grebstein, Sheldon. "The Comic Anatomy of Portnoy's Complaint". *Comic Relief: Humor in Contemporary American Literature*. Ed. Sarah Blacher Cohen. Urbana: U of Illinois P, 1978. 152-71.

Green, Martin. "Half a Lemon, Half an Egg." Milbauer and Watson 73-81.

——. Introduction. *A Philip Roth Reader*. By Philip Roth. London: Vintage, 1993. IX-XXIII.

Gross, John. "Marjorie Morning Star, Ph.D." *New Statesman* 30 Nov. 1962: 784. Rpt. in Pinsker 40-43.

Guttman, Allen. "Jewish Humor." *The Comic Imagination in American Literature*. Ed. Louis D. Rubin. New Brunswick, NJ: Rutgers UP, 1973. 329-38.

Hicks, Granville. "A Bad Little Good Girl." Rev. of *When She Was Good*, by Philip Roth. *Saturday Review* 17 June 1967: 25-26.

Hochman, Baruch. "Child and Man in Philip Roth." *Midstream* 13 (Dec. 1967): 68-76.

Howe, Irving. "Philip Roth Reconsidered." *Commentary* Dec. 1972: 69-77. Rpt. in Pinsker 229-44.

Hyman, Stanley Edgar. "A Novelist of Great Promise." *The New Leader* 11 June 1962: 22-23. Rpt. in Pinsker 36-40.

Isaac, Dan. "In Defense of Philip Roth." *Chicago Review* 17 (Fall/ Winter 1964): 84-96. Rpt. in Pinsker 182-93.

Israel, Charles M. "The Fractured Hero of Roth's *Goodbye, Columbus*." Critique: *Studies in Modern Fiction* 16 (Dec. 1974): 5-11.

Kundera, Milan. "Some Notes on Roth's *My Life as a Man* and *The Professor of Desire*." Milbauer and Watson 160-67.

Landis, Joseph C. "The Sadness of Philip Roth: An Interim Report." *The Massachusetts Review* 3 (Winter 1962): 259-68. Rpt. in Pinsker 164-71.

Larner, Jeremy. "The Conversion of the Jews." *Partisan Review* 27 (Fall 1960): 760-68.

Lee, Hermione. "Kiss and Tell." *New Republic* 30 Apr. 1990: 39-42.

Leonard, John. "Fathers and Ghosts." *New York Review of Books*. Oct. 25, 1979: 4.

Levitt, Morton P. "Roth and Kafka: Two Jews." Pinsker 245-54.

Lewis, Cherie S. "Philip Roth on the Screen." *Studies in American Jewish Literature* 8 (Fall 1989): 186-95.

Lyons, Bonnie. " 'Jew on the Brain' in 'Wrathful Phillipics'." *Studies in American Jewish Literature* 8 (Fall 1989): 154-67.

Mabbot, John David. "History of Ethics." *Encyclopaedia Britannica*, 1968 ed.

Monaghan, David. "*The Great American Novel* and *My Life as a Man*: An Assessment of Philip Roth's Achievement." *International Fiction Review* 2 (1975): 113-20. Rpt. in Pinsker 68-77.

Mudrick, Marvin. "Who Killed Herzog? or Three American Novelists." *University of Denver Quarterly* 1 (1966): 61-97.

Nelson, Gerald B. "Neil Klugman." *Ten Versions of America*. New York: Knopf, 1972. pp. 147-62.

Novak, Estelle Gershgoren. "Strangers in a Strange Land: The Homelessness of Roth's Protagonists." Milbauer and Watson 50-72.

Podhoretz, Norman. "Laureate of the New Class." *Commentary* Dec. 1972: 4.

Prescott, Peter S. "Roth in Full Flower." *Newsweek* Sept. 10, 1979: 72-73.

Raban, Jonathan. "The New Philip Roth." *Novel* 2 (Winter 1969): 153-63.

Sabiston, Elizabeth, "A New Fable for Critics: Philip Roth's *The Breast*." *International Fiction Review* 2 (1975): 27-34.

Shechner, Mark. "Jewish Literature." *Harvard Guide to Contemporary American Writing*. Ed. Daniel Hoffman. Delhi: Oxford UP, 1981. 191-239.

——. "Philip Roth." *Partisan Review* 41 (Fall 1974): 410-27.Rpt. in Pinsker 117-32.

Sheed, Wilfred. "Howe's Complaint." *New York Times Book Review* May 6, 1973: 2.

Siegel, Ben. "The Myths of Summer: Philip Roth's *The Great American Novel*." *Contemporary Literature* 17 (Spring 1976): 171-90.

Sinclair, Clive. "The Son Is the Father to the Man." Milbauer and Watson 168-79.

Solotaroff, Theodore. "The Journey of Philip Roth." *Atlantic* Apr. 1969: 64-72.

Solotaroff, Theodore. "Philip Roth and the Jewish Moralists." *Chicago Review* 13 (Winter 1959): 87-99. Rpt. in *Contemporary American-Jewish Literature: Critical Essays*. Ed. Irving Malin. Bloomington: Indiana UP, 1973. 13-29.

Tucker, Martin. "The Shape of Exile in Philip Roth, or the Part is Always Apart." Milbauer and Watson 33-49.

Vanderbilt, Kermit. "Writers of the Troubled Sixties." *Nation* Dec. 17, 1973: 661-65.

Voelker, Joseph C. "Dedalian Shades: Philip Roth's *The Ghost Writer*." Pinsker 89-94.

Walden, Daniel. "*The Professor of Desire:* The Two Plums or the Reawakening?" Pinsker 78-82.

Watson, Donald G. "Fiction, Show Business, and the Land of Opportunity: Roth in the Early Seventies." Milbauer and Watson 105-25.

Whitfield, Stephen J. "Laughter in the Dark: Notes on American-Jewish Humor." *Midstream* Feb. 1978: 48-58. Rpt. in Pinsker 194-208.

Wirth-Nesher, Hana. "From Newark to Prague: Roth's Place in the American-Jewish Literary Tradition." Milbauer and Watson 17-32.

Wolf, Geoffrey. "Beyond Portnoy." *Newsweek* Aug. 3, 1970: 66-67.